DATE DUE

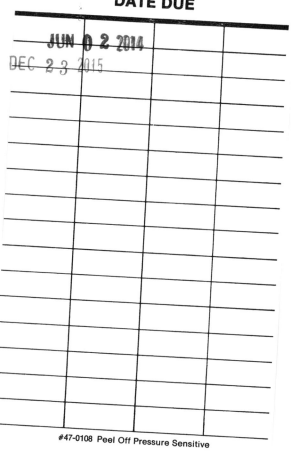

JUN 0 2 2014		
DEC 2 3 2015		

#47-0108 Peel Off Pressure Sensitive

STREPTOCOCCUS (GROUP B)

DEADLY DISEASES AND EPIDEMICS

DEADLY DISEASES AND EPIDEMICS

STREPTOCOCCUS (GROUP B)

Tara C. Smith, Ph.D.

FOUNDING EDITOR
The Late I. Edward Alcamo
Distinguished Teaching Professor of Microbiology,
SUNY Farmingdale

FOREWORD BY
David Heymann
World Health Organization

CHELSEA HOUSE
PUBLISHERS
An imprint of Infobase Publishing

Deadly Diseases and Epidemics: *Streptococcus* **(Group B)**

Chelsea House
An imprint of Infobase Publishing
132 West 31st Street
New York, NY 10001

Library of Congress Cataloging-in-Publication Data
Smith, Tara C., 1976–
  Streptococcus (group B) / Tara C. Smith ; consulting editor I. Edward Alcamo ; foreword by David Heymann.
    p. ; cm. — (Deadly diseases and epidemics)
  Includes bibliographical references and index.
  ISBN-13: 978-0-7910-9243-9 (alk. paper)
  ISBN-10: 0-7910-9243-7 (alk. paper)
  1. Streptococcal infections. 2. Streptococcus. I. Title. II. Series.
  [DNLM: 1. Streptococcal Infections. 2. Streptococcus agalactiae—pathogenicity. WC 210 S662s 2007]
  RC116.S84S6559 2007
  616.9'298—dc22   2007006966

Text design by Terry Mallon
Cover design by Takeshi Takahashi
Illustrations by Sholto Ainslie
Printed in the United States of America
Bang EJB 10 9 8 7 6 5 4 3 2 1
This book is printed on acid-free paper.

Table of Contents

Foreword

In the 1960s, many of the infectious diseases that had terrorized generations were tamed. After a century of advances, the leading killers of Americans both young and old were being prevented with new vaccines or cured with new medicines. The risk of death from pneumonia, tuberculosis (TB), meningitis, influenza, whooping cough, and diphtheria declined dramatically. New vaccines lifted the fear that summer would bring polio, and a global campaign was on the verge of eradicating smallpox worldwide. New pesticides like DDT cleared mosquitoes from homes and fields, thus reducing the incidence of malaria, which was present in the southern United States and which remains a leading killer of children worldwide. New technologies produced safe drinking water and removed the risk of cholera and other water-borne diseases. Science seemed unstoppable. Disease seemed destined to all but disappear.

But the euphoria of the 1960s has evaporated.

The microbes fought back. Those causing diseases like TB and malaria evolved resistance to cheap and effective drugs. The mosquito developed the ability to defuse pesticides. New diseases emerged, including AIDS, Legionnaires', and Lyme disease. And diseases which had not been seen in decades reemerged, as the hantavirus did in the Navajo Nation in 1993. Technology itself actually created new health risks. The global transportation network, for example, meant that diseases like West Nile virus could spread beyond isolated regions and quickly become global threats. Even modern public health protections sometimes failed, as they did in 1993 in Milwaukee, Wisconsin, resulting in 400,000 cases of the digestive system illness cryptosporidiosis. And, more recently, the threat from smallpox, a disease believed to be completely eradicated, has returned along with other potential bioterrorism weapons such as anthrax.

The lesson is that the fight against infectious diseases will never end.

In our constant struggle against disease, we as individuals have a weapon that does not require vaccines or drugs, and that is the warehouse of knowledge. We learn from the history of science that "modern" beliefs can be wrong. In this series of books, for example, you will learn that diseases like syphilis were once thought to be caused by eating potatoes. The invention of the microscope set science on the right path. There are more positive lessons from history. For example, smallpox was eliminated by vaccinating everyone who had come in contact with an infected person. This "ring" approach to smallpox control is still the preferred method for confronting an outbreak, should the disease be intentionally reintroduced.

At the same time, we are constantly adding new drugs, new vaccines, and new information to the warehouse. Recently, the entire human genome was decoded. So too was the genome of the parasite that causes malaria. Perhaps by looking at the microbe and the victim through the lens of genetics we will be able to discover new ways to fight malaria, which remains the leading killer of children in many countries.

Because of advances in our understanding of such diseases as AIDS, entire new classes of antiretroviral drugs have been developed. But resistance to all these drugs has already been detected, so we know that AIDS drug development must continue.

Education, experimentation, and the discoveries that grow out of them are the best tools to protect health. Opening this book may put you on the path of discovery. I hope so, because new vaccines, new antibiotics, new technologies, and, most importantly, new scientists are needed now more than ever if we are to remain on the winning side of this struggle against microbes.

David Heymann
Executive Director
Communicable Diseases Section
World Health Organization
Geneva, Switzerland

1

The Emergence of Group B Streptococcal Disease

Nothing is ever static when it comes to infectious **disease**. Bacteria are able to reproduce incredibly quickly—as fast as within 20 minutes under ideal circumstances. This reproduction is never quite perfect. Each generation of bacteria may go through **mutations** (inheritable changes) in its **DNA**, changing the new generation slightly from its parent population of bacteria. These mutations may be harmful, beneficial, or neutral. They may be changes in single **nucleotides** of the DNA code (the chemicals that make up the DNA chain) or they may be large additions or removals of pieces of DNA. In some cases, a bacterium may even acquire a large chunk of DNA that carries **virulence genes** (genes that help make a bacterium cause disease) or even **antibiotic resistance**, allowing the bacterium to grow even in the presence of drugs that would typically kill it. Together, these mutations may allow one population of bacteria to outcompete another in an ever-changing ecological landscape. Keeping on top of the changing threats of infection in newborn infants is a major challenge to pediatricians. For many years in the late nineteenth and early twentieth centuries, group A streptococcus bacteria (*Streptococcus pyogenes*) was a major cause of **meningitis** (inflammation of the brain) and **sepsis** (blood infections) in **neonates** (newborn infants). In the 1940s, these streptococci were largely replaced by **coliform** organisms (a group of organisms found in fecal material of animals). The coliforms were briefly supplanted by severe infections caused by *Staphylococcus* in the late 1950s, but then returned to prominence. In 1961, a published report showed that the group B streptococcus (*Streptococcus agalactiae*, or GBS—short for "group B streptococcus") played an important role in **perinatal** (the period around childbirth) problems of a mother and her infant in New Orleans. This was followed by a report that described two instances of meningitis in neonates that were also caused by this same organism. By the early 1970s, group B streptococcus was recognized as a leading cause of neonatal infection. It has retained that status ever since.

HISTORY OF GROUP B STREPTOCOCCUS

Group B streptococcus was originally identified in 1887 by Norcard and Mollereau as a cause of bovine (cow) **mastitis**

WHAT IS AN "EMERGING DISEASE"?

An emerging disease is defined by the Centers for Disease Control (CDC) as "any of a group of diseases, of various cause, that have newly appeared or are rapidly expanding their range in the human species." These can include viruses, bacteria, fungi, or other organisms that are completely new to scientists—organisms such as the Marburg and Ebola viruses discovered in the 1960s and 1970s, or HIV in the 1980s. Emerging diseases can also include organisms that were known but were typically not believed to infect humans (such as GBS before the 1970s) or organisms that have been fairly benign in the past but suddenly become a problem to human health when they acquire virulence factors or antibiotic resistance genes through mutations. Pathogens that are new to a particular geographic area may also be labeled as "emerging" diseases. The West Nile virus is a recent example of this phenomenon: Until the late 1990s, it had never been seen in the United States, and now it has spread throughout the country. Emerging diseases are such a problem that the CDC has dedicated an entire journal to research in that area: *Emerging Infectious Diseases*.

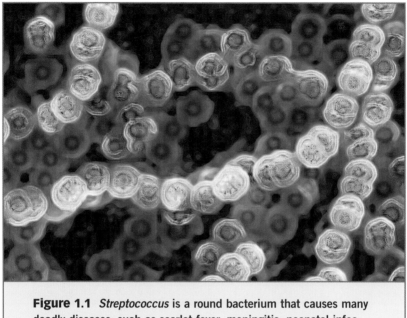

Figure 1.1 *Streptococcus* is a round bacterium that causes many deadly diseases, such as scarlet fever, meningitis, neonatal infection, and pneumonia. (James Cavallini/Photo Researchers, Inc.)

(inflammation of the mammary glands). However, until the early 1930s, streptococcal bacteria were generally separated into two groups: **beta-hemolytic** (causing **lysis**, or breaking apart, of red blood cells) and nonhemolytic (unable to cause lysis). In 1933, American bacteriologist Rebecca Lancefield divided streptococcal bacteria into a number of groups based on a **carbohydrate** found on the bacterial cell surface: group A, which were infections of humans; group B, which were infections of cattle; group C, which affected various animals; group D, which affected cheese; group E, which affected milk, and so on. Even as she established these classifications, however, scientists knew that these groups were only broad generalizations and not strict delineations. A report by English researchers Ronald Hare and Leonard Colebrook in 1934 showed that streptococci could be isolated from the genital tract of 10 percent of the women they tested. Most of the *Streptococcus* strains they found were similar to those isolated from bovine mastitis. In 1940, Arthur Hill and Hildred Butler similarly reported that the group B streptococcus *Streptococcus agalactiae* caused approximately 10 percent of the cases of **puerperal sepsis** (a bacterial infection of the blood following birth) in their hospital in Australia. Despite these reports and many others, most scientists still tended to discount the clinical importance of human group B streptococcal infections for many decades.

Although it was generally unfamiliar to pediatricians before it rose to prominence in the 1970s, between 1930 and 1960 there were occasional reports of severe GBS disease in infants. In 1973, several **prospective** studies were published in the *Journal of Pediatrics*, clarifying the link between GBS and infant mortality. One study by Ralph Franciosi and colleagues at the Medical College of Wisconsin found an **incidence** (rate

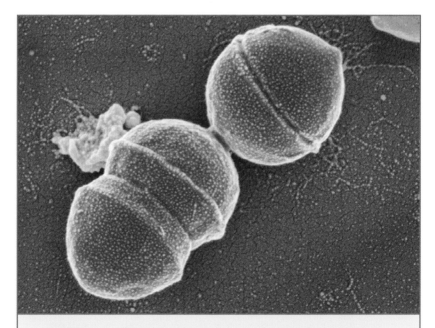

Figure 1.2 *Streptococcus* (group B) or *streptococcus agalactiae* is the primary cause of bacterial infection in newborn babies. (Dr. Gary Gaugler/Photo Researchers, Inc.)

of new infections) in newborns of two infections per 1,000 live births. The bacterium causes neonatal sepsis and meningitis. Of the infected infants, approximately half died, giving the disease a 50 percent **mortality rate**. Franciosi and his fellow researchers also found that a significant proportion of both women and men were **colonized** (carrying the bacteria but showing no **symptoms**) with GBS anally and/or vaginally (for women). Similar results (with a lower mortality rate) were reported by Leslie Barton and colleagues at the University of Arizona. A paper by American researcher Carol Baker and others showed that there was a difference between **early-onset** (in infants less than 10 days old) and **late-onset** (in infants between 11 days and 12 weeks old). Even with all these studies, it took many years for GBS to be listed in medical microbiology textbooks as more than a cause of bovine mastitis and occasional infection of humans.

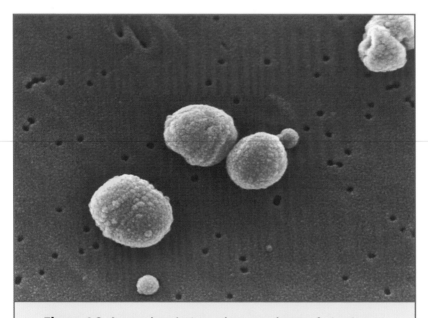

Figure 1.3 A scanning electron microscope image of *streptococcus pneumoniae*. (CDC/Janice Carr)

HOW IS GBS RELATED TO OTHER STREPTOCOCCI?

Species in the genus *Streptococcus* are among the most common disease-causing Gram-positive bacteria. In addition to *Streptococcus agalactiae*, the genus *Streptococcus* also includes group A streptococcus (*Streptococcus pyogenes*), which is a common cause of pharyngitis (strep throat). Another common human pathogen is *Streptococcus pneumoniae*, which causes pneumonia and is also a frequent cause of otitis media (ear infections). Although these three are the most notable streptococci when it comes to human disease, there are more than a dozen other species of streptococci. Species of streptococci are frequently divided into two groups: beta-hemolytic (causing the destruction of red blood cells in a blood agar plate, leading to a clear zone around the bacterial colony) and nonbeta-hemolytic. The first group includes group A and B streptococci as well as group C and G streptococci. Group C streptococci include several species, such as *Streptococcus equi*, a pathogen of horses and other animals. (*S. equi* can also infect humans on rare occasions.) Group G streptococci include *Streptococcus canis*, which typically infects dogs.

Of the nonbeta-hemolytic streptococci, *Streptococcus pneumoniae* is the species that causes most human disease. This bacterium is a leading cause of pneumonia (infection of the lungs) and it has become increasingly resistant to antibiotics. A vaccine is available that has proven effective in children. It reduces the severe disease caused by this bacterium in children under the age of five, and in adults older than 65, two groups at highest risk of death from pneumonia. Other nonbeta-hemolytic streptococcal species include *Streptococcus mutans*, *Streptococcus oralis*, *Streptococcus gordonii*, and *Streptococcus salivarius*, all of which are oral bacteria that play a role in periodontal disease.

WHAT CAUSED THIS EMERGENCE?

No one knows for sure why GBS seemed to suddenly become a major cause of neonatal infections in the 1970s. It has even been suggested that no real "emergence" occurred. Neonatal infections with GBS were sporadically documented in the professional literature, though this appears to be a fairly rare phenomenon until the 1970s. It was suggested that the "emergence" is simply a recognition **bias**—that is, as reports of finding these bacteria in diseased infants increased in that decade, more people began to look for the bacteria. With more people looking, more infections were diagnosed. **Retrospective** (looking into the past) analyses make this scenario unlikely, however, as researchers were unable to find GBS in patient samples that had been stored. Therefore, there is no evidence that GBS infections were routinely missed prior to the 1970s.

Some researchers have suggested that a change in the routine cleansing of newborns may have played a role in

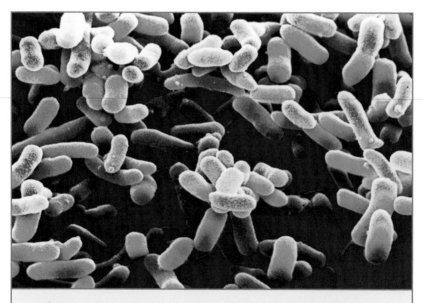

Figure 1.4 *E. coli.* (Dr. David M. Phillips/Visuals Unlimited)

the emergence of GBS infections. From around 1960 until 1972, many hospitals employed a procedure to fight bacterial infections in newborns. Newborn infants were bathed in a 3 percent hexachlorophene solution, a chemical that kills bacteria, just after birth. This was done to reduce the number of **Gram-positive** bacteria on the skin, leaving primarily **Gram-negative** organisms. (In the years before the emergence of GBS as a neonatal pathogen, the most common organism that caused neonatal infections was *Escherichia coli* [*E. coli*], a Gram-negative bacterium [Figure 1.4]). Some hospitals reported high mortality from GBS infection even in the early 1960s, but it is not known whether those hospitals were using the hexachlorophene procedure at the time. Perhaps a mutation in one population of GBS made it better able to cause disease in newborns. Perhaps the ecology of bacteria carried by humans changed in some way, allowing GBS to either infect more people or to reproduce to higher numbers in the humans they infected, thereby increasing the likelihood that the bacteria would be transferred to others. Though these are interesting hypotheses, the data to support or confirm them are lacking. They have been lost in time. Unfortunately, we may never know why GBS so quickly became a key cause of neonatal infections in the United States. We can, however, focus on the present and do all we can to prevent other bacteria from emerging in the same way.

2

Microbiology and Epidemiology of GBS

Streptococcus agalactiae is a Gram-positive **coccus**. This means that it contains a cell wall thick with a chemical called **peptidoglycan** and is shaped like a sphere. Typically, these bacteria grow together in chains. A group of them looks something like a string of pearls when viewed through a microscope.

GBS can be divided into nine groups based on the outer **capsule**, a sticky coating on the outside of the bacterium. The capsule is made of **polysaccharide** (complex sugar) that protects the bacterium from **dessication** (drying out) and other environmental hazards. These nine groups are referred to as **serotypes**, since they have traditionally been identified using **antisera** (a portion of the blood containing **antibodies**—host proteins that recognize particular polysaccharides) against the capsule types. GBS has been divided into serotypes Ia, Ib, and II through VIII. Combined, serotypes Ia, II, III, and V cause up to 90 percent of all cases of GBS infection in the United States.

COLONIZATION AND RISK FACTORS

Most studies of colonization with GBS have been carried out in populations of pregnant women. These types of studies have increased recently with the recommendation of universal screening of pregnant women for colonization with GBS (see Chapter 4). Therefore, it is difficult to apply the results from these studies to the general population. Nevertheless, research on pregnant women can provide some insight into GBS colonization. Several studies have found higher rates of colonization in African-American and Hispanic women than in Caucasian women. However,

Caucasian women have been found to be more likely to be colonized with serotype V GBS. Serotype V is more likely to be resistant to the antibiotics erythromycin and clindamycin than other serotypes, which is discussed later in this chapter.

Additional colonization studies have been carried out in a population of college students at the University of Michigan. The studies found that approximately 34 percent of women and 21 percent of men were colonized with GBS. Of the **isolates** collected, the most common serotype was serotype V (29 percent), followed by serotype III (20 percent). Serotypes Ia and Ib each made up 12 percent of the collected isolates. Again, because the University of Michigan student population does not necessarily represent the population at large, these results cannot easily be extended to the rest of the populace.

WHAT IS A "DISEASE?"

The terminology used in science and medicine can be confusing at times. For example, *disease* and *infection* are often used as synonyms, although they are actually two separate things. We are all constantly "infected" by an immense number of different organisms, but they rarely cause disease. An infectious disease is characterized by infection with a microbial agent, along with symptoms that relate to that infection. The infectious agent may cause these symptoms, or they may be due to the reaction of the body's immune system to the infection. A fever, for example, is a reaction of the immune system. It is caused by the release of chemicals called cytokines that act to raise the core body temperature. The infecting agent itself may also cause symptoms. The scarlet fever rash caused by *Streptococcus pyogenes*, for instance, is caused by the production of a toxin. An infection that causes no symptoms (and, therefore, no obvious disease) is called a subclinical or asymptomatic infection (sometimes referred to as a subclinical or asymptomatic disease).

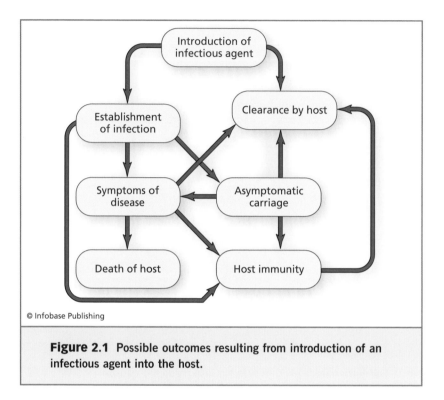

Figure 2.1 Possible outcomes resulting from introduction of an infectious agent into the host.

GBS INFECTION IN NEONATES

In the United States, serotype III GBS has traditionally been associated with serious disease in neonates. Approximately 80 percent of these infections occur within the first few days of life. This is termed early-onset disease. Neonates who come down with early-onset disease were infected **intrapartum** by their mothers, who were colonized with GBS in the genital tract. From there, the GBS enters the amniotic fluid. The neonate may then inhale this fluid. This type of transmission (directly from the mother to the neonate) is termed **vertical transmission**.

IS GBS SEXUALLY TRANSMITTED?

When one thinks of sexually transmitted diseases, names such as gonorrhea, syphilis, and AIDS generally come to mind. Many other infectious agents, however, can be transmitted by sexual contact. Some of these cause serious disease in a large number of those who get infected. Others, however, rarely cause any disease at all. The human papillomavirus (HPV), for example, is a sexually transmitted infection that causes genital warts in a small percentage of infected individuals. It may also lead to cervical cancer in some women. Despite this, most people who are infected never show any symptoms.

This appears to be the case with GBS as well. Although relatively few individuals show symptoms of infection with GBS, many of us carry the bacterium, and one way it appears to be transmitted is via sexual contact.

A 2005 report describes a case of "honeymoon meningitis." A woman entered the emergency room complaining of fever, headache, and vomiting. Suspecting meningitis, doctors gave her antibiotics and collected a sample of her cerebral spinal fluid (CSF) in order to test it for bacteria. The CSF and blood samples both showed the presence of GBS. It turned out that the young woman had recently been married and had had her first sexual experience two days before going to the emergency room. GBS were also found in her vagina.

A study led by Leslie Meyn at the University of Pittsburgh showed that sexual activity was correlated with GBS colonization in a study of more than 1,200 women. Another study found that 18 husbands of 40 GBS-positive women were colonized with the same serotype of GBS. A study published in 2004 found that among 57 couples in which at least one partner carried GBS, 86 percent were colonized with the same strain. A different study found that the strongest predictor of GBS colonization was a history of sexual activity.

Late-onset disease occurs in infants between 11 days and two to three months of age. In some cases, the bacterium may be acquired from the mother; in other cases, it is unclear how the neonate becomes infected. It is possible that the bacterium is transferred from a caregiver's contaminated hands to the child.

Screening for GBS during the final months of pregnancy, followed by antibiotic treatment during labor, has reduced the incidence of early-onset disease significantly in the past decade. In 1996, the average incidence of early onset GBS disease was 1.8 cases per 1,000 live births. By 1998, the incidence was reported to average 0.6 cases per 1,000 live births—a 66 percent reduction. Currently, this means there are approximately 1,600 early-onset cases and 80 deaths each year due to GBS. However, although early-onset GBS cases have decreased, late-onset disease has remained relatively constant, averaging approximately 0.4 cases per 1,000 live births over the past decade. Further studies are needed to determine how late-onset infection might be avoided.

SIGNS AND SYMPTOMS OF EARLY-ONSET GBS DISEASE

Serotype III isolates are commonly associated with neonatal infections. A 1998 report showed that 36 percent of early-onset neonatal infections and 71 percent of late-onset infections were caused by serotype III. With early-onset infections, most newborns will exhibit symptoms within the first 24 hours of life, often as soon as the first hour after birth. This rapid onset suggests that GBS infection develops **in utero** (within the womb before birth), and that many newborns are already infected when they are born. The particular disease that the newborns will develop from GBS depends on where the bacterium grows in the body. Most will have **septicemia** (bacteria in the blood), which is present approximately 80 percent of the time; pneumonia (bacteria in the lungs), which occurs about 7 percent of the time; and/

or meningitis, which happens about 6 percent of the time. Other potential sites of infection include the skin and other soft tissues, the cardiovascular system, the urinary tract, eyes, and gastrointestinal tract.

Symptoms in the newborn vary, but the most common sign of GBS disease is respiratory distress (difficulty breathing). Newborns may also be **lethargic** (tired and sleepy), may feed poorly, and may have an unstable body temperature. Severe difficulty breathing, low blood pressure, and seizure may follow these symptoms. Early-onset disease has a high mortality rate. Even when it is cured, it can result in permanent disabilities, including mental retardation and loss of hearing and/or vision. Mortality rates range between 4.5 percent and 15 percent, depending on the age of the infant and the treatment provided.

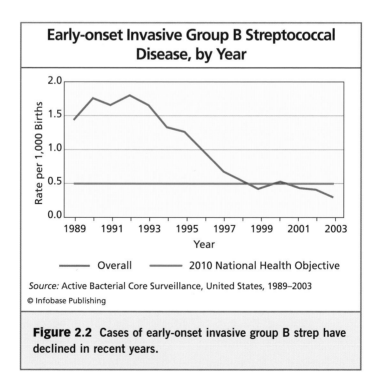

Early-onset Invasive Group B Streptococcal Disease, by Year

Source: Active Bacterial Core Surveillance, United States, 1989–2003
© Infobase Publishing

Figure 2.2 Cases of early-onset invasive group B strep have declined in recent years.

LATE-ONSET GBS DISEASE IN INFANTS

Infants who develop late-onset GBS disease do not show symptoms until after the first week of life, sometimes as late as two to three months of age. As a result, GBS may not initially be suspected as the problem. Symptoms of late-onset disease are often nonspecific—that is, they are symptoms that could be caused by a number of different bacteria and viruses. The symptoms include lethargy and poor feeding, similar to what is seen with early-onset disease; irritability; fever; and ear infections. A larger portion of infants with late-onset than early-onset disease will develop meningitis: 30 percent–40 percent of infants with late-onset disease will develop this dangerous condition.

Late-onset disease can also have what is called a "focal presentation": The infection is limited to one part of the body. For example, it may show up as facial **cellulitis**, a skin infection that appears more often in male than female infants. It may cause arthritis in any of the joints. Case reports show that the bacteria may be localized in almost any organ of the body. Mortality from this type of infection ranges from approximately 2 percent to 6 percent. As mentioned above, the incidence of late-onset GBS disease has not changed despite the widespread use of intrapartum antibiotic treatment.

GBS DISEASE IN ADULTS

Although infants are generally the most commonly mentioned at-risk group for the development of serious GBS disease, adults also can develop the disease. Often GBS disease in adults occurs as septicemia, and adults who are **immunocompromised**—have a weakened immune system, often due to other conditions, such as cancer, diabetes, or AIDS—are at a higher risk of developing GBS disease.

GBS infection can lead to other types of serious GBS disease. Among these is a disease called **streptococcal toxic shock-like syndrome** (STSS). This is a condition characterized by the sudden onset of fever, **hypotension** (low blood pressure), vomiting, diarrhea, and **shock** (failure to maintain adequate blood volume and flow to organs). A rash may occur as well. Most commonly, this type of syndrome is caused by *Staphylococcus aureus* or *Streptococcus pyogenes*, which are group A streptococci. However, GBS is increasingly being recognized as a cause of this syndrome as well. It appears to be caused by a toxin produced by certain isolates of GBS, which leads to the rash and, ultimately, to the other symptoms (and possibly death). Research suggests that, if this trend continues, we are likely to see more cases of STSS due to GBS in the future.

In addition to STSS, GBS can cause a spectrum of other diseases in adults. These include urinary tract infections, cellulitis, wound infections, pneumonia, meningitis, and **endocarditis**. GBS can also cause a highly fatal condition called **necrotizing fasciitis**, often referred to as "flesh-eating disease." This is a rare, severe infection that involves the **subcutaneous** tissues. Although only a handful of cases of necrotizing fasciitis due to GBS were reported over the past four decades, a surge in these types of cases has been reported in the past 10 years.

THE EMERGENCE OF SEROTYPE V

Although serotypes Ia and III are the most common sero-types of GBS in infants, serotype V isolates have increasingly been found in adults. Serotype V was first identified by a retrospective analysis in 1975, and it was found at a low rate in the 1970s and 1980s. In the 1990s, however, identification of serotype V GBS increased dramatically. In 1992, serotype V isolates accounted for 2.6 percent of all GBS isolates. In 1993, they accounted for 14 percent, and 20 percent in 1994. This increase remains unexplained, although studies have shown that it is not the result of an introduction of a single invasive **clone**. In other words, a single serotype V bacterium did not spread throughout the country; rather, several different sero-type V strains have been found. Many serotype V isolates, however, have been found to be resistant to the antibiotics erythromycin and clindamycin. This may allow them to out-compete other GBS isolates carried by a host who is exposed to antibiotics.

Serotype V has also been isolated from serious invasive diseases. One study in Taiwan, for example, found that almost one-third of isolates recovered from soft tissue infections in adults were serotype V. Many of these infections led to amputations of infected limbs; death occurred in 7 percent of cases.

WILL SEROTYPE VIII EMERGE IN THE UNITED STATES?

Serotype V isolates of GBS were not often found in the United States before the early 1990s, even though they were present in the population since at least 1975. Although the factors causing this emergence are currently unknown, researchers are looking closely at other virulent serotypes that may represent a similar threat. The most likely candidates are currently serotype VIII isolates. These are not commonly found in the United States, but serotype VIII is a dominant serotype in Japan, often found in pregnant women. In addition, it has emerged as an invasive pathogen in Denmark, making up 6 percent of all invasive GBS isolates in 2002. Invasive serotype VIII isolates have also been found in Australia and the state of Maryland, whereas colonizing serotype VIII isolates have been identified in Korea and in the city of Boston, Massachusetts. Several studies have suggested that serotype VIII isolates may be less virulent than isolates of other serotypes and, therefore, less likely to cause the high mortality rate that serotype V has caused. Bacteria, however, are a moving target—although they may now be less virulent, no one knows what the future may bring. The acquisition of virulence factors or antibiotic resistance could dramatically change the epidemiology of these isolates. Only time and careful surveillance will tell.

PREVENTION OF INFECTION

The old adage "An ounce of prevention is worth a pound of cure" certainly holds true when it comes to GBS infection. Culturing women while they are pregnant and treating those who are known to be colonized with this bacterium during labor has dramatically reduced the incidence of early-onset disease in newborns. The rate of late-onset disease, however, has not changed. Ideally, a vaccine will eventually be made available to protect people of all ages against GBS disease.

3

Diagnosis and Treatment

Traditionally, a GBS infection has been defined by the isolation of a GBS organism from an otherwise **sterile** site, such as blood or spinal fluid, but there are a number of problems with this type of diagnosis. First, it is often difficult to determine whether the person had a true infection with GBS or a nonthreatening colonization. Many people are colonized with GBS—we carry the bacterium as a **commensal** organism that does not harm us. It may be present as part of the normal bacteria in the gastrointestinal tract or vagina (in women). In some cases, it may even be present on the skin or in the throat. It is only when the bacteria breaches one of our natural defenses and enters a site where bacteria are normally not present, such as the bloodstream, that the bacterium becomes a pathogen—an organism that causes harm.

TESTING FOR GBS

A number of tests can be used to diagnose and identify GBS. First, one needs to collect a sample from the body. This is done by placing swabs (which look like long Q-tips) into the vagina or rectum. These swabs are then swished around in a liquid containing two antibiotics: gentamicin and nalidixic acid. These antibiotics allow GBS to grow but kill most other bacteria. To allow the bacteria to grow, the liquid is then incubated overnight at 37°C (98°F). A portion of this is then plated on a **blood agar plate**—a gelatin-like substance containing 5 percent sheep's blood to aid in bacterial growth. These are again grown overnight at 37°C. The next day, the scientist can examine the bacterial colonies on the plate. GBS generally appears as white colonies surrounded by a zone of transparent agar. These colonies can then be identified to determine which serotype they are. This will distinguish them from other related streptococci (such as *Streptococcus pyogenes*), which can look similar on a blood agar plate.

Another test that is frequently used is the CAMP test. (CAMP stands for Christie, Atkins, Munch, and Petersen—the last names of the people who discovered this method.) For this test, an isolate of *Staphylococcus aureus* that produces a protein called the beta toxin (ß-toxin) is streaked across a blood agar plate. Suspected strains of GBS are then streaked on the same plate, perpendicular to *Staphylococcus aureus*. A positive CAMP test will result in an arrowhead-shaped hemolysis zone near the intersection of *Staphylococcus aureus* and *Streptococcus agalactiae*, while a negative test will lack this arrow shape.

Although colony color and shape and protein expression tests (including the CAMP test and others) have historically been the most common methods to diagnose GBS infections,

Figure 3.1 *Bacillus cereus*, a Gram-positive beta-hemolytic bacteria showing on sheep blood agar. (CDC/Courtesy of Larry Stauffer, Oregon State Public Health Library)

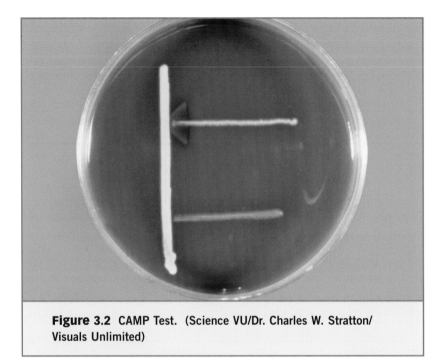

Figure 3.2 CAMP Test. (Science VU/Dr. Charles W. Stratton/ Visuals Unlimited)

molecular methods (looking directly at the DNA) are increasingly being used instead of bacterial culture. These tests have the advantage of being quicker and, in some cases, cheaper than culture-based techniques. These tests are either based on the polymerase chain reaction (PCR, a DNA-based test that amplifies a portion of the GBS chromosome), or proteins produced specifically by the bacterium. These tests can be carried out in a few minutes to a few hours (versus one to several days for older methods), allowing for more rapid diagnosis and application of an appropriate treatment.

TREATMENT

Treatment for GBS varies according to age group. Infants are usually put on the antibiotic ampicillin, along with an **aminoglycoside** such as gentamicin while laboratory work is done to confirm the diagnosis of GBS infection. This combination of antibiotics is referred to as "broad spectrum." It is effective not only against GBS but also against other common bacterial causes of neonatal disease, such as *Escherichia coli*, *Listeria monocytogenes*, and *Enterococcus faecalis*. If no bacteria grow, antibiotics can be stopped after two days—the patient is not infected with GBS. If the infant tests positive for GBS, an antibiotic called penicillin G is the preferred drug for treatment. Because many people are allergic to penicillin, however, a second antibiotic (ampicillin) may be used instead. One problem is that up to 12 percent of women may be resistant to penicillin; in these women, clindamycin and erythromycin may be used as alternative antibiotics. Antibiotics are typically administered for two weeks.

ANTIBIOTIC RESISTANCE

The antibiotic of choice for treating GBS infections is penicillin, the first antibiotic discovered. Incredibly, GBS isolates remain almost universally susceptible to penicillin, despite more than 60 years of using the antibiotic to treat diseases. No one is quite sure why this is the case, especially since other pathogenic organisms quickly developed resistance to penicillin. Whatever the case, penicillin remains a fairly cheap and effective drug for the treatment of serious GBS disease. The biggest downside is that approximately 10 percent of the population is allergic to penicillin and cannot take the drug.

Other drugs have not fared as well as penicillin. A 2003 study carried out in an obstetrics and gynecology (OB/GYN) clinic in Ohio sampled 200 GBS isolates from 2001 to 2004, looking for resistance to the antibiotics erythromycin and clindamycin. The study found exceptionally high levels of resistance to both antibiotics. Of these 200 strains of GBS, 107 of them (54 percent) were resistant to erythromycin, while 66 (33 percent) were resistant to clindamycin. All the clindamycin-resistant strains were also resistant to erythromycin.

The isolates in this study were taken from vaginal and/or rectal samples of pregnant women. Therefore, they were **carriage** isolates: portions of each woman's normal bacterial

flora, rather than isolates that were currently causing disease. These high rates of resistance to erythromycin and clindamycin were also found in a 2004 study carried out by Shannon Manning and others at the University of Michigan. A group of college students were sampled and GBS was isolated from vaginal, rectal, throat, or urine samples. As in the Ohio study, these GBS isolates were carriage isolates that were not currently causing disease. Of the individuals sampled, 29 percent carried GBS resistant to erythromycin, while 18 percent carried clindamycin-resistant isolates. A larger study carried out by the same researchers found similar results. Like the Ohio study, all the clindamycin-resistant strains were also resistant to erythromycin. These resistance rates were approximately

HOW DOES ANTIBIOTIC RESISTANCE EMERGE?

Drugs used to treat bacterial infections are called antibiotics. The discovery and widespread availability of these drugs is a hallmark in the battle against infectious disease. They allow humans to survive infections that, previously, had resulted either in certain death, or potential amputation of infected limbs.

This victory, however, has come with a cost. Many bacteria have become increasingly resistant to antibiotics: The drugs no longer work against them. This resistance has resulted from a number of different factors. One is overuse of antibiotics. Antibiotics are not only used to treat infections, but also are given to livestock in order to improve growth. Because these antibiotics are used at low doses, they generally are not concentrated enough within the animal to kill large numbers of bacteria. Instead, they kill those that are most susceptible to the drugs, leaving behind bacteria that are better able to resist the drugs.

A second factor contributing to the increase in antibiotic resistance is simple genetics. The genes that are responsible double those found in a study performed two years earlier in the same area among pregnant women.

In contrast, a 2005 study from Germany found a much lower rate of resistance to these antibiotics. The German researchers found that, overall, 11 percent of their 338 GBS isolates were resistant to erythromycin, and only 4.7 percent were resistant to clindamycin. This difference might be due to geographic differences, or to the fact that a greater percentage of the German isolates were from invasive infections rather than carriage. Either way, it is certain that antibiotic resistance in this species of bacterium is of grave concern, and one that has the potential to compromise the health of many vulnerable populations.

for providing bacteria with resistance to antibiotics often are found on circles of DNA called plasmids. These plasmids can be transferred between bacteria, so even a bacterium that is susceptible to an antibiotic can become resistant with the acquisition of a plasmid containing an antibiotic resistance gene. These can spread from animals to humans via the food we eat, or due to contact with manure or other products from animals harboring antibiotic-resistant organisms.

Finally, although animals are one source of antibiotic-resistant bacteria, they are other places where these bacteria can be found. Hospitals are also sources for these bacteria. Patients not only bring antibiotic-resistant bacteria into the hospital with them, but also the bacteria can be transferred among existing patients via nurses, hospital beds and bedding, and even medical equipment. Even more worrisome is the fact that some of these bacteria, such as a strain of *Staphylococcus* that is resistant to multiple antibiotics, are increasingly being found and spread within the community as well.

PHAGE THERAPY

Resistance to antibiotic treatment is a concern with GBS and other bacterial pathogens. One strategy to remedy the resistance problems is to continuously develop new antibiotics, so there is always a drug available to which the bacteria will be susceptible. This is like playing a "cat and mouse" game, with humans always one step behind bacteria. Therefore, it is wise to try alternative strategies, in addition to developing new drugs. Vincent Fischetti of The Rockefeller University is trying to do precisely that. His strategy involves using one microbe to kill another.

Figure 3.3 Vincent Fischetti of Rockefeller University. (Courtesy Vincent Fischetti)

Fischetti has used a group of proteins called lysins that kill bacteria by digesting the bacterial cell wall, making cells susceptible to breaking open. These lysins come from another class of microorganisms—viruses called bacteriophages. These are viruses that actually infect bacteria, including GBS. In a 2005 study, Fischetti showed that a lysin from a GBS bacteriophage—a virus that specifically infects GBS—could be used to get rid of GBS from the vagina and oropharynx (mouth and throat) in a mouse. It is possible that this technique could be used instead of antibiotics to treat pregnant women and stop GBS colonization just prior to birth. It may also prove useful in eliminating GBS from the mouth and throat of newborns, as it is believed that bacteria from these regions are most likely to cause meningitis. It remains to be seen whether Fischetti's treatment will ever come into widespread use, but it is certainly an example of the innovative thinking that will be needed to compete with the growing number of antibiotic-resistant bacteria.

4

GBS with Pregnancy and Other Conditions

In the early 1970s, a series of reports demonstrated the emergence of group B streptococcus (GBS) as the leading cause of neonatal sepsis and meningitis in the United States. Once attention had been drawn to the problem, researchers began to study what the **risk factors** were for the disease—that is, what was different about the groups of infants who developed GBS disease compared to those who didn't? To investigate this, scientists used a **case-control study**. Researchers identified women whose infants were diagnosed with disease caused by *Streptococcus agalactiae* and compared them with women whose infants did not have the disease. If there were differences, perhaps the researchers could find a target for intervention and reduce the incidence of GBS disease.

A number of differences were found following many different studies. One important risk factor was the duration of membrane rupture. You

Table 4.1 **Risk Factors for GBS**

Premature delivery (less than 37 weeks gestation)
Intrapartum fever (above 100.4°F)
Rupture of membranes 12 hours or more prior to delivery
GBS bacteruria (bacteria in the urine) during pregnancy
A previous newborn with a GBS infection
Rectal or vaginal cultures that test positive for GBS

STUDY DESIGNS

Scientists who study disease patterns are called epidemiologists. In order to investigate these diseases, they use a number of different kinds of studies.

A study that starts in the present and proceeds forward in time is called a prospective study. For example, if a researcher wants to examine the effect of a certain drug on a condition, he or she may follow a group of subjects (called a cohort) for a number of years to determine whether the drug is successful in treating a disease and if it causes any side effects (adverse reactions). This is a prospective cohort study.

A retrospective study may be used to examine the effect that past events or exposures have on disease development. Researchers may notice a cluster of cancer cases in a town. From this, they may identify cases (those who have been diagnosed with the disease) and controls (those who show no signs of the disease). They could then examine differences in past exposures between these two groups. Perhaps the cases lived in the same area or consumed the same drinking water that was later found to be contaminated with a chemical, while the controls drank from a different source. This type of study is called a "retrospective case-control" study.

The choice of study design depends on different factors. One is cost: Cohort studies are generally more expensive than case-control studies, and they often involve larger numbers of individuals. Prospective studies also tend to cost more money, since the researcher needs to follow the chosen group for a number of months or years in order to obtain accurate records. Retrospective studies tend to cost less, because the scientist can pick out those with the desired outcome (such as the development of a particular disease) and then match controls to them, so that each group has approximately the same makeup of age, race, and other variables. In the end, whichever research study design is chosen, the goal is the same: to better understand human health and the factors that lead to the development of disease.

may have heard someone say that a woman's "water broke" before she gives birth. What this really refers to is the rupture of the membrane containing the **amniotic fluid**, a liquid that surrounds and protects the fetus inside the amniotic sac within the uterus. Many more infants who suffer from early-onset GBS disease had mothers whose membranes ruptured longer than 12 hours before delivery than infants who did not have the disease. Therefore, an extended amount of time between membrane rupture and delivery appears to be a risk factor for GBS disease.

Infants who were delivered vaginally had higher rates of GBS disease than those delivered by **cesarean section** (a procedure in which the fetus is delivered through an incision in the abdomen rather than through the birth canal). Therefore, vaginal delivery appears to be a risk factor.

One difference between the groups that appeared to protect infants from development of GBS disease was intrapartum antibiotic use: administering antibiotics that are effective against GBS intravenously during labor.

The observation that intrapartum antibiotics appeared to protect infants from developing GBS disease led to extensive testing of this antibiotic **prophylaxis** (treatment with antibiotics prior to the onset of infection) to prevent deaths from GBS. In the early 1980s, clinical trials began by administering antibiotics to mothers at high risk of disease. These trials were successful in preventing early-onset GBS disease. This led to an increased awareness of GBS as a fatal disease that could be prevented. In the 1990s, the CDC and American College of Obstetricians and Gynecologists (ACOG) published guidelines for intrapartum antibiotic use, in order to prevent the vertical transmission (transmission from mother to child via the birth canal) of GBS. Initially, candidates for receipt of antibiotics were selected based on risk factors for GBS disease (Table 4.1). In 2002, these guidelines were modified slightly, recommending that health-care

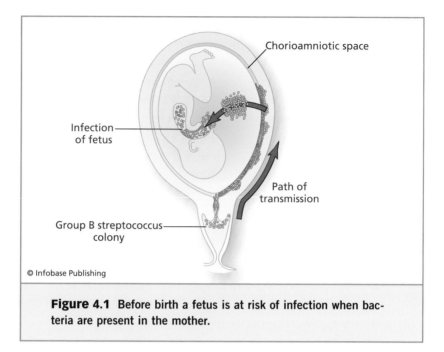

Chorioamniotic space

Infection
of fetus

Path of
transmission

Group B streptococcus
colony

© Infobase Publishing

Figure 4.1 Before birth a fetus is at risk of infection when bacteria are present in the mother.

providers screen all pregnant women for GBS colonization between the 35th and 37th weeks of pregnancy. Recent clinical trials, however, have suggested that the administration of antibiotics to pregnant women may be associated with adverse neonatal problems, including **necrotizing enterocolitis** (a gastrointestinal disease that can destroy part or all of the infant's intestine) or an increased need for supplementary oxygen. Currently, approximately 35 percent of mothers receive antibiotics during labor.

Early-onset GBS infection is caused by vertical transmission, in which the bacterium enters the **chorioamniotic space** (the space between the two membranes that enclose the fetus—the **chorion** and the **amnion**) before birth (Figure 4.1). Approximately 50 percent of newborns of mothers who are colonized with GBS will be exposed to GBS either by the rupture of membranes or through the vaginal birth process.

INTRAPARTUM ANTIBIOTICS

Intrapartum antibiotic use has been credited with a significant decrease in the incidence of severe GBS disease in newborns in the first week of life. This benefit, however, could come with other costs. Although one 2005 study found no increase in antibiotic-resistant GBS since the start of intrapartum antibiotic use, a new study suggests that the use of antibiotics may have serious consequences for some infants.

Prior to the 1970s, the major cause of neonatal bacterial infections was Gram-negative organisms such as *Escherichia coli*. In the mid 2000s, several reports have noted an increase among neonatal infections in premature infants due to antibiotic-resistant Gram-negative organisms. In a study published in the journal *Pediatrics*, Tiffany Glasgow and colleagues at the University of Utah investigated whether this increase could be due to maternal antibiotic therapy. Although the use of the appropriate antibiotics would kill any GBS that are present, organisms that are resistant to the antibiotics would survive and could even take over niches left open when susceptible bacteria were killed. Glasgow found that the infants of mothers who received ampicillin or other broad-spectrum antibiotics were more likely to develop a subsequent infection with an antibiotic-resistant pathogen.

Based on this information, what should a physician recommend to a pregnant woman? First, Glasgow's study suggests that broad-spectrum antibiotics should not be used unless they are absolutely necessary. Physicians should ask mothers about a history of intrapartum antibiotic administration from prior births when they see a case of early-onset bacterial infection in neonates. The best way to prevent GBS disease in infants would be to have an effective vaccine, eliminating the need for antibiotics.

Only 1 percent to 2 percent of these infants will go on to develop severe disease.

Risk factors associated with late-onset disease have not been well defined. Vertical transmission from the mother followed by a delayed onset is one possibility. **Nosocomial transmission** (hospital-based transmission) is another option: The mother, father, nurses, or other handlers of the newborn may carry the bacterium and transmit it to the baby, resulting in disease.

SEROTYPES ASSOCIATED WITH NEONATAL INFECTIONS

Experiments carried out over a decade ago by Jim Musser and colleagues at the Baylor College of Medicine suggested that, in serotype III isolates, most invasive strains clustered within two distinct types. The study found that 95 percent of 44 invasive serotype III isolates clustered into one of two groups, based upon the proteins expressed. More recent studies into the epidemiology of serotype III isolates have suggested they can be divided into three subgroups (III-1, III-2, and III-3) based on DNA analysis. The researchers found that the majority of invasive isolates from neonates were type III-3. Type III-3 also has unique phenotypic features: Isolates showed a lag in growth in chemically defined medium supplemented with phosphate, poor growth at 40°C (104°F), a significantly higher amount of sialic acid production (a component of the bacterial capsule), and a decreased likelihood to produce C5a peptidase, a virulence factor that will be discussed further in Chapter 6. Recently, Elisabeth Adderson and colleagues at St. Jude's Research Hospital in Memphis, Tennessee, found a gene specific to these III-3 species: the *spb1* gene (surface protein of group B *Streptococcus* 1). *Spb1* has been found to help the bacterial cells attach to and invade host cells, and it has been suggested as a potential vaccine candidate.

GBS AND OTHER CONDITIONS

Although GBS disease is most often discussed in terms of pregnancy and infants, nonpregnant adults can also be infected. As mentioned in Chapter 3, approximately 30 percent of adults carry GBS either in their gastrointestinal tract, vagina, or throat. Those who are healthy and have strong immune systems are able to keep growth of the bacteria in check, but those who are elderly or have weakened immune systems may not be so lucky. Infections in nonpregnant adults account for more than 75 percent of GBS disease, and this number appears to be growing.

A recent retrospective study conducted in Spain examined 150 cases of GBS disease. It found that 39 percent of the cases were in adults who had diabetes, and another 23 percent were in patients who had cancer. When the type of infection was examined, 42 percent of all patients had infections of the skin and soft tissue. Of these, more than 50 percent were patients who also had diabetes. The study also found that the incidence of GBS infection and **bacteremia** in adults increased during the study period (1993–2000). In 1993, the incidence of GBS disease was 0.53 per 1,000 hospital admissions; the incidence of bacteremia was 0.15 per 1,000 admissions. By the year 2000, the incidence of GBS disease had almost doubled to 0.96 per 1,000 admissions, with bacteremia similarly increasing to 0.42 per 1,000 admissions. In a similar study carried out in Atlanta, Georgia, it was found that greater than 40 percent of young adults with invasive GBS infection had diabetes.

GBS IN THE ELDERLY

Susceptibility to blood-borne bacterial infections increases with advancing age. Currently, adults age 65 and older account for more than 40 percent of cases and approximately two-thirds of the deaths attributable to GBS in the United States each year. Indeed, GBS fatality rates in the elderly are higher than in neonates: 13 percent of elderly patients die, compared with a 3 percent–5 percent death rate for infected neonates.

Epidemiological studies have shown that, among the elderly, infections with GBS of serotype V are increasingly common. First identified in the early 1990s, serotype V now accounts for approximately 24 percent to 31 percent of disease-causing isolates in nonpregnant adults. A study by Rene Amaya and others at the Baylor College of Medicine showed that the elderly who were examined lacked an antibody that was specific to the serotype V GBS capsule. Another Baylor study in 2005 conducted by Morven Edwards and others showed that, of colonized elderly individuals, approximately 50 percent were colonized with serotype V GBS. This combination of low antibody prevalence and high colonization rates is potentially deadly.

GBS IN THOSE WITH OTHER CONDITIONS

In addition to the elderly, GBS affects those with other underlying conditions, such as diabetes and cancer, much more frequently than it does the young and healthy. In a number of studies, **diabetes mellitus** has been found to be the most frequent underlying condition in adult GBS patients, with cancer of some type the second most frequent. This information is especially worrisome in light of recent data that show that rates of diabetes in the United States are rapidly increasing. Currently, approximately 7 percent of the U.S. population has diabetes, and this number is rising due to the aging population and increasing levels of obesity.

Other conditions have also been associated with an increased risk of invasive GBS disease. These include **cirrhosis** and history of stroke. As the population ages and these conditions become increasingly common, will this mean more infections with GBS? It seems likely, although it is difficult to say for sure. It would be a terrible shame to gain valuable years in infants whose GBS disease was prevented, only to lose them to adults with diabetes on whom GBS takes a significant toll.

5

GBS Infection in Animals

IS GBS A ZOONOTIC PATHOGEN?

GBS was long thought to cause only bovine mastitis (infection of the mammary glands). Scientists did not think it caused disease in humans. We now know that GBS is a significant cause of infection and disease in humans, but it remains a major pathogen of cattle as well. Bovine mastitis is the major cause of economic loss to the dairy industry through reduced milk yield and quality, cost of drugs and veterinary treatment, and discarded milk. These problems cost the dairy industry approximately $2 billion every year.

Many researchers study GBS in the bovine population, focusing largely on the epidemiology, evolution, and presence of antibiotic resistance within the cattle population. When GBS was first found to be a human pathogen, scientists wondered whether GBS was a **zoonotic disease**, one that is transmitted between different animal species. Examples of zoonotic pathogens include rabies, *Ebola* virus, and *Escherichia coli*.

A number of studies have investigated this question over the years. Despite a large amount of research, the question has not been answered satisfactorily. Over the past five years, investigations increasingly have used a molecular method called **multi-locus sequence typing** (MLST). In MLST, the DNA sequences of a number of **housekeeping genes** in each bacterial isolate are determined. Housekeeping genes are involved in functions that are critical for cell survival, such as nutrient utilization and DNA repair. From the nucleotide sequences of these housekeeping genes, the investigator can determine how closely related the isolates being studied are. One study by Naiel Bisharat and others at the Ha'Emek Medical Center in Israel using MLST suggested that a particular type of GBS—a serotype III clone that is responsible for many cases of neonatal disease—originally came from a bovine strain. Perhaps this was the reason for the emergence of GBS into the human population in the 1970s—a bacterium from cattle became established in humans. Future studies will investigate this hypothesis.

Using somewhat different methods and different bacterial populations, other investigators have also found that some human GBS populations have a bovine ancestor. John Bohnsack and colleagues at the University of Utah examined serotype III isolates taken from bovine milk and from human neonatal infections. Instead of using MLST, they sequenced a gene called *infB*, which previous studies had found to be useful in examining the epidemiology of GBS. Bohnsack's results, like

Figure 5.1 A laboratory worker conducts a PFGE test. (CDC/ James Gathany)

Bisharat's, suggested that this deadly strain of GBS arose from a recent bovine ancestor.

Does this mean that GBS is, in fact, a zoonotic disease? The answer is yes and no. It appears that, at the very least, one lineage of neonatal serotype III was transmitted to humans by cattle. Another reason to carefully monitor GBS in cattle is to look for the presence of antibiotic resistance in this population of bacteria. Resistance to a number of key antibiotics is increasing in GBS, and cattle may be one source for these resistant GBS—potentially transmitting resistance bacteria to the human population.

PFGE

Pulsed-field gel electrophoresis (PFGE) is a technique used to differentiate bacterial isolates. To use this procedure, the DNA of each isolate is extracted and cut with a restriction enzyme—a protein that cuts DNA at specific spots. There are dozens of known restriction enzymes, which have been isolated from a number of different bacterial species. Each of them has a unique cutting "signature." For example, the enzyme *EcoRI*, isolated from *Escherichia coli*, always looks for the DNA sequence GAATTC in any stretch of DNA. When it finds this, it will cut the DNA between the G and A, leading to two DNA fragments instead of one. This is repeated over the chromosome, until the DNA is cut up into small pieces.

Once the DNA has been cut, it is loaded into a gel made of agarose—a substance similar to hardened gelatin. An electric current is then pulsed through the gel, which causes the DNA to move from one end of the gel to the other. Because of their size, the larger chunks of DNA get stuck in the pores at the top of the gel, while the smaller pieces continue through toward the end. A "ladder" contain-

GBS IN OTHER ANIMALS

GBS has been found in a wide variety of animals besides humans and cattle. Several reports have told of finding GBS in sick dogs, including one case of endocarditis (an infection inside of the heart). Previous studies have also reported that GBS may be associated with neonatal deaths in puppies.

One 1998 study examined the molecular characteristics of GBS isolated from a dog, cat, and monkey. All were found to be closely related to human GBS isolates. Were these isolates transmitted to the animals from a human source? Again, this is a question researchers have been unable to answer.

ing DNA pieces of a known size is also loaded into the gel, so that the sizes of the DNA fragments from the sample can be determined. The gel, with its DNA portions still inside, is then stained with a chemical called ethidium bromide. It is then visualized using UV light. The DNA pieces show up as white bands. The positions of these bands can be used to determine how closely related two bacterial isolates are. Two isolates that are identical or very closely related will have the same or a similar PFGE pattern. Less closely related isolates will have different banding patterns.

By analyzing the band patterns along with other information about the bacterial isolate, researchers can tell whether two strains are related. This is particularly important in an outbreak situation, since isolates with the same banding pattern tend to have a common source.

PFGE can also be used to determine whether an isolate from an infant is the same as one from the mother, which would suggest that the infant was infected by vertical transmission. PFGE is a useful tool for rapidly determining the epidemiological relationships among a group of bacterial isolates.

Some interesting GBS transmissions have, however, been clearly documented. A 2003 publication reported the deaths of three adult emerald monitor lizards that died due to infection with GBS (Figure 5.2). These lizards were fed a diet of mice. When the intestinal bacteria of the remaining mice were examined, GBS was found. The isolates from the mice and the isolates taken from the deceased lizards were typed using pulsed-field gel electrophoresis (PFGE) and found to be identical. Therefore, Udo Hetzel and his colleagues at the Institute for Veterinary Pathology in Giessen, Germany, concluded that the monitor lizards acquired the bacteria from their diet of GBS-infected mice.

GBS is also considered an emerging disease in numerous fish species. In fish, GBS can cause a serious, often fatal, septicemia. GBS has also been isolated several times from horses and has been found in the udders of camels and ewes (female sheep). GBS has even been found to cause sores on the feet of male elephants.

Figure 5.2 Emerald monitor lizard. (David A. Northcott/Corbis)

It is easy to see that GBS has an incredibly broad range, infecting not only various species of mammals, but also cold-blooded vertebrates such as lizards and fish. Unfortunately, the critical question—whether GBS is a zoonotic disease—remains unanswered. This will only be determined by careful and extensive studies, examining isolates from humans, cattle, and a wide variety of animal species. However, this type of study requires a significant investment of money and resources.

6

Virulence Factors

Despite approximately 30 years of study, relatively little is known about important **virulence factors** in GBS, which are genes that, when present, allow an organism to cause disease. Some established and potential virulence genes that have been identified will be discussed below.

GBS CAPSULE

A capsule is the sticky polysaccharide that surrounds a bacterium. It has long been considered an important virulence factor. The capsule allows the bacterium to avoid being killed by certain types of immune system cells. The bacterial capsule (the sticky, protective covering) exists in at least nine different types of GBS: Ia, Ib, and II through VIII. Six genes involved in capsule expression have been identified: *cpsA through cpsF*.

C ANTIGEN

The first surface protein **antigen** identified in GBS was the c antigen. This protein is actually composed of two unrelated protein components: the alpha protein, or α protein, (encoded by the *bca* gene) and the ß protein (encoded by the *bac* gene). Strains reported to express the c antigen may express either the α protein, the ß protein, or both. These antigens are sometimes, but not often, found in invasive serotype III strains. They are more commonly found in serotypes Ia, Ib, and II strains.

The α protein has previously been shown to be **immunogenic** (meaning it causes our immune system to react). The ß protein appears to play a role in helping the bacterium hide from the host immune system. The ß protein is found in almost all strains of serotype Ib and in a few of the serotypes Ia, III, and V. It is very rarely found in serotype III. Though strains that express the ß protein usually also express the ß protein, the ß protein can also be expressed alone, especially in strains of serotype Ia.

RIB PROTEIN

Whereas the c antigen is sometimes found in serotype III isolates, another surface protein, Rib (encoded by a gene called "rib"), is frequently found in these strains. Both of these antigens are part of the Alp (alpha-like protein) family. These proteins all have an extended region made up of long, completely identical repeats of amino acids (the building blocks of proteins).

SEROTYPES, STRAINS, AND ISOLATES

When discussing bacteria, the terminology can sometimes get confusing. When discussing GBS, the serotype is the most inclusive group. In GBS, there are nine different serotypes: Ia, Ib, and serotypes II-VIII. Therefore, all the bacteria in this species can be subdivided into one of these nine serotypes.

Below serotype is the strain. A strain of bacteria means that they share a very similar genetic background; that they are very closely related. Strains are then made up of bacterial isolates. Each individual bacterium taken from a person, an animal, or the environment is an isolate.

One way to think of this is like a box of crayons. You can divide crayons into a few basic colors: red, orange, yellow, green, blue, purple, brown, black, white. These are similar to the serotype designation for bacteria. The various shades within each color (burgundy, aquamarine, lime green) would correspond to the strains of bacteria. Even if you have 10 boxes of crayons, you can still group all the burgundy ones together. Each individual crayon, then, would be an isolate. Though it's closely related to the other burgundy crayons, one may have come from Minnesota and another one from Florida, making them distinct isolates within the same strain.

In addition to serotype III, Rib is expressed by a number of serotype II strains. It is also occasionally found in serotype V strains.

LAMININ-BINDING PROTEIN

The laminin-binding protein is a surface protein that is present in almost all strains of *Streptococcus agalactiae*. Researchers have suggested that it plays a role in colonizing the host and possibly in invading damaged epithelial cells. Laminin-binding protein is encoded by the *lmb* gene, and is similar to a protein expressed in the group A streptococcus.

SIP

The Sip protein is another protein on the surface of GBS. Sip was identified in GBS of all known serotypes. Its specific function is not known, however, and it has not been firmly established as a virulence gene.

SPB1

A deadly strain of GBS associated with neonatal infections has been identified. Using a number of genetic techniques, investigators determined that these invasive serotype III isolates are closely related and have placed them in a subtype of serotype III (designated serotype III-3). What makes this lineage more dangerous than other serotype III isolates? Elisabeth Adderson et al. of St. Jude Research Hospital asked this question in a 2003 paper. When they compared a harmless GBS strain with one of these dangerous serotype III-3 isolates, they found a gene that was present only in the dangerous one. They named this gene *spb1*, which stands for "surface protein 1 of the group B streptococcus."

When the *spb1* gene was "knocked out" (rendered nonfunctional) in a serotype III-3 isolate, the knock-out mutant's ability to adhere to and invade human epithelial cells was reduced. When the *spb1* gene was added to a noninvasive serotype III-2 isolate, the virulence of the III-2 isolate increased, suggesting that the *spb1* gene may indeed act as a virulence factor. Additional studies need to be carried out to better understand the role this protein may play in virulence.

C5A PEPTIDASE

During an infection, the host may respond by producing a molecule called C5. This is cut by a protein called a C5a convertase (essentially a protein that splits the C5 molecule into two parts) into C5a and C5b. C5b is then used to poke holes in and kill invading bacterial cells. C5a, on the other hand, works to recruit cells of the immune system called **neutrophils** to the site of infection. The neutrophils then eliminate the infecting bacteria. During a GBS infection, this immune response is often reduced or absent because GBS produces a molecule that cleaves and inactivates C5a. That molecule is called **C5a peptidase**. It is a protease (a protein that cuts other proteins apart) encoded by the *scpB* gene.

covR/S

Recently, a gene has been identified that appears to regulate a number of virulence factors in *Streptococcus agalactiae*. This locus, called *covR/S*, is a two-component regulatory system. These consist of two proteins that work together. The first senses a change in the environment (for example, the level of sugar in the environment), while the second sends a signal to other genes in order to coordinate a response to this change. This kind of system is common in bacteria, and the locus in GBS is very similar to one in the group A streptococcus, *Streptococcus pyogenes*.

A number of these two-component systems have been found in GBS, but *covR/S* is the only one that has been extensively investigated. *CovR/S* has been found to control the expression of a large number of other GBS genes. *CovR/S* is called a "global regulator" of GBS gene expression, since expression (or lack thereof) of these genes results in an increase or decrease in expression of a large number of other GBS genes, kind of like a universal light switch.

HOW DIVERSE ARE BACTERIA?

How much diversity can be present in a bacterial population? Many species of bacteria are DNA scavengers; they pick up pieces of DNA from the environment through a process called horizontal (or lateral) gene transfer. Some bacteria take these new pieces up easily—they are said to be "naturally transformable." With others, it's more difficult for new DNA to get in. In many cases, bacteriophages—viruses that infect bacteria—may bring in new genes when they infect a bacterium. However they're introduced, this sharing of genes in bacteria is extremely common.

All this transfer can sometimes complicate examinations of bacterial phylogeny (evolutionary history and relatedness of species). In a 2005 paper by Hervé Tettelin and colleagues, the authors sequenced six new isolates of GBS (that is, they determined the entire string of DNA base pairs that made up the genome of each of the six isolates). They compared all these, plus two other isolates that had been sequenced before. It was found that the eight isolates shared a "core genome" of around 1,800 genes. The interesting part of the research, however, was when they looked at the unique genes in each isolate. The sum of all the core plus all the unique genes in the species has been termed the pan-genome: the total amount of genes present in the entire bacterial species. With eight isolates sequenced, the researchers tried to see if they could estimate the size of this "pan-genome" in order to get an

ROGB

Another regulatory gene in GBS is the *rogB* gene. It controls a number of potential virulence factors within the bacterium, including genes involved in helping the bacterium adhere to host cells. *RogB* was also found to positively regulate expression idea of how many isolates would have to be sequenced to capture the extent of the total genetic diversity in GBS. Using their model, they concluded that, for every new GBS genome sequenced, they would find an average of 33 new strain-specific genes to add to the pan-genome—therefore, the GBS pan-genome is, essentially, unending.

Is an "infinite diversity" of genes even available? Critics argue that the researchers were premature to extrapolate their numbers from only eight isolates. The researchers acknowledge this problem. This diversity is really not so surprising, however. Despite the recognition of bacteria as disease-causing agents well over 100 years ago, we know amazingly little about these organisms. The Institute for Genomic Research (TIGR) has made some huge leaps forward, sequencing genomes of more than 1,800 predicted species and finding 1.2 million new genes from the Sargasso Sea, and playing a role in the investigation into the diversity of the bacteria in the human intestine. In that study, they determined that, of about 400 phylotypes (closely related bacterial species), fully 80 percent of them were from species that hadn't even been cultured yet. A similar situation exists with human oral bacteria—many species, of which we have no knowledge, exist within our own mouths. With this much bacterial diversity merely in these unexamined microbes within our bodies, who knows how much is out there in the environment?

of another gene, called *fbsA*. This gene encodes the FbsA protein, which binds to the human cellular protein fibrinogen. This protein has also been suggested to play a role in **quorum sensing** in the bacterium. Quorum sensing is a way of recognizing and responding to changes in bacterial population density.

BACTERIAL BIOFILM

In the laboratory setting, scientists typically study bacteria as a pure culture: A single colony of the bacterium is grown and expanded—reproducing a million clones of itself, so that all the bacteria in the solution are, essentially, exactly the same. In nature, however, this rarely happens. Most of the time, bacteria live in a complex matrix consisting of multiple bacterial species along with fungi or yeast, human cells, and macromolecules such as polysaccharides and DNA. All these organisms, when they adhere to a surface, are called a biofilm. They are everywhere: on your shower curtain, in your sink, even in your mouth. You know them more commonly as "soap scum" or "plaque," but, when examined at a microscopic level, they include various species of bacteria.

Bacteria growing in a biofilm may be protected from several environmental stresses. Because a sticky, poorly permeable coating surrounds them, they are less susceptible to antibiotics and other destructive chemicals. Because of this physical coating, they can also avoid exposure to host antibodies or other defenses, making them exceedingly difficult to treat. In fact, it has been estimated that 65 percent of nosocomial (hospital-acquired) infections are associated with biofilm. In the United States alone, these bacteria cost billions of dollars each year to treat and result in thousands of deaths.

Generally, biofilm bacteria are nonmotile; they do not move. They grow very slowly and have less access to nutrients than bacteria grown in a laboratory. These attributes make them very difficult to treat, because most antibiotics target bacterial proteins that are produced only when bacteria are actively growing (which represent only a small portion of all the bacteria in a biofilm). Therefore, bacteria that are not in the process of growth—the majority of the biofilm—will be resistant to antibiotic treatment.

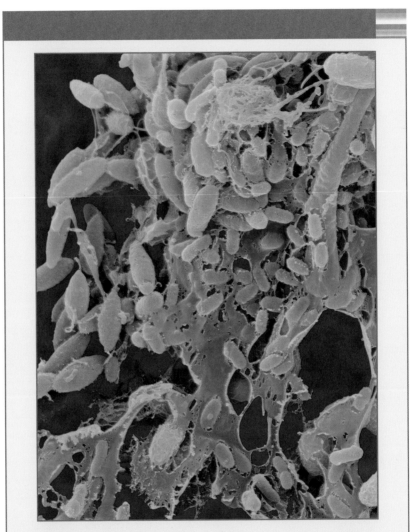

Figure 6.1 Bacteria growing on a biofilm. (Dr. Dennis Kunkel/ Visuals Unlimited)

Only one study so far has examined the growth of GBS in a biofilm. It found that when this bacterium was grown in a biofilm, it was much more resistant to a number of antibiotics than bacteria grown in typical culture media.

HEMOLYSIN

GBS is beta-hemolytic: It causes a clear zone of lysis when grown on an agar plate containing blood. Researchers have recently found that the protein that causes this **phenotype** (physical appearance) is linked to the production of a **carotenoid** pigment; that is, that the hemolysin and a pigment protein are expressed at the same time. This is an orange pigment that is present in many isolates of GBS that acts as an **antioxidant**: It protects the bacterium against oxidative damage, such as that caused by the cells of the human immune system. This pigment is related to ß-carotene, the pigment that gives carrots their orange color (and makes them healthy for us to eat). Both of these phenotypes have been linked to the recently identified *cylE* gene. Studies are ongoing to further understand the role of these proteins.

7

Vaccine Prospects

Although the incidence of early-onset GBS disease has decreased over the past decade, the incidence of late-onset GBS disease in infants has remained unchanged. Adults in several groups (especially the elderly and those with diseases such as diabetes) remain at high risk for the development of invasive GBS disease—including healthy adults with no underlying health conditions. Furthermore, screening and treatment during pregnancy and labor is expensive, administration of antibiotics during labor is an invasive procedure that poses its own risks, and, as noted in Chapter 3, antibiotic resistance within the bacterial population is increasing. Although screening has reduced the number of deaths caused by GBS, it is far from an ideal solution. An inexpensive, effective vaccine would be a much better way to prevent GBS disease. Laboratory data have shown that the absence of antibodies to the GBS capsule polysaccharide correlates with the development of invasive GBS disease. An increase in antibody levels in many individuals in the population, as occurs with the use of vaccines, should serve to decrease the amount of new invasive GBS infections. Currently, most work on investigating potential GBS vaccines has focused on the polysaccharide capsule as a key antigen.

CAPSULE-BASED VACCINES

There are currently nine known capsular serotypes of GBS. Five of these are common in the United States and Europe; others are more common in other regions (serotype VIII, for example, is common in Japan). Therefore, any capsule-based vaccine would need to contain multiple antigens, in order to provide protection against more than one serotype of GBS.

Capsule-based vaccines, however, present a few key challenges. Most notably, the capsule serotypes responsible for invasive GBS disease may change over time—for example, due to immunity to a particular serotype in the general population, or acquisition of new virulence genes or antibiotic resistance genes by the bacteria. Over the past 20 years, most research has focused on serotype III, because it has been the most prominent serotype responsible for invasive disease in neonates. Other serotypes continue to be identified, however, and their significance in the development of severe invasive disease may be changing. For instance, serotype V was virtually never found before the early 1990s, when it more commonly caused invasive disease in healthy adults. Today, it represents as much as 30 percent of GBS in some geographic areas. This change highlights the need for monitoring strains of GBS, both before and after a vaccine is implemented.

In addition, because the capsule antigen is a carbohydrate—essentially, a sugar—the antigen is poorly immunogenic. In other words, the antigen does not spark a vigorous immune system reaction as some other antigens (such as proteins) do. One way scientists can get around this feature of carbohydrates is to couple them with a protein—link them together—in a vaccine. That way, the protein will make the immune system react more vigorously, providing better protection against the disease. Several studies have examined the effect of capsule antigens joined with a protein called **cholera toxin B** with some success. Research suggests that this may be a way to exploit the capsule antigens as potential vaccine candidates.

Since the initial recognition of antibodies directed at the capsule, more than 20 trials have been carried out using vaccines that contain capsule antigens from GBS. These trials have had various degrees of success. A 2004 study by Debra Palazzi and others at the Baylor College of Medicine, for example, examined a vaccine based on a serotype V capsule joined with tetanus **toxoid** in adults 65 to 85 years old. This vaccine was found to cause significant levels of anticapsule **immunoglobulin** (called IgG) to be produced in those who received it, which suggested that the vaccine may work to prevent GBS disease caused by this serotype. Since GBS infections in the adult population are frequently caused by serotypes Ia and III in addition to V, a capsule-based vaccine would need to include antigens for these capsule types as well. Also, this vaccine was tested in healthy elderly people. Many elderly people who develop GBS disease have underlying conditions, such as cancer or diabetes, that make them more susceptible. The vaccine was not tested in these groups, so its usefulness remains uncertain. Because of these and other limitations with capsule-based vaccines, researchers have looked elsewhere for GBS vaccine candidates.

GBS SURFACE PROTEINS

A number of surface-attached and secreted (released from the bacteria) proteins that are thought to play a role in the **pathogenesis** of GBS infections were described in Chapter 6. Many of these have also been investigated for use in a GBS vaccine, either alone or in combination with other proteins. One problem with these surface proteins as vaccine candidates is that none has been found in a large majority of isolates. Therefore, as with a capsular-based vaccine, a number of different surface protein antigens would need to be included to create an effective vaccine.

One of the first antigenic proteins described in GBS was the c antigen, a protein composed of either the α protein, the ß protein, or both (see Chapter 6). Rebecca Lancefield and others at Rockefeller University showed in 1975 that antibodies to the c antigen provided protection against infection with GBS in mice. These findings appeared to be largely ignored, however, perhaps because the c protein is not commonly found in the invasive serotype III isolates.

One surface protein that has been investigated as a potential vaccine candidate is the Rib protein. This protein was tested in mice, using a number of different methods. Rib protein alone was injected into mice subcutaneously (below the skin); other groups of mice received Rib protein along with an inactivated cholera toxin and were treated **intranasally**—through the nose. A third group of mice was untreated. When the mice were then injected with a lethal dose of GBS bacteria, more survived in the immunized groups than the nonimmunized group. Of the immunized mice, a larger percentage of those immunized with the Rib protein injected subcutaneously survived than those immunized intranasally using the Rib/cholera toxin combination. Although the trial was successful, a drawback to the use of Rib as a vaccine is that it is present in only approximately 25 to 30 percent of isolates—however, it is often found in the highly invasive serotype III isolates that are most commonly associated with neonatal infection.

Perhaps the most promising protein vaccine candidate is a protein called Sip. In neonatal mice, a vaccine using this protein has been shown to protect against a number of GBS strains from various serotypes, including isolates of serotype Ia, Ib, II, III, and V—the most common serotypes in the United States. Additionally, the antibodies produced in response to this protein were shown to cross the placenta—meaning that mothers could be vaccinated with this protein and the immunity to GBS would pass to the fetus. Further studies need to be conducted to test this idea.

IS A UNIVERSAL VACCINE POSSIBLE?

The best of all possible options would be a single-component vaccine that would provide a high level of protection against all strains of GBS. A 2005 paper published in the journal *Science* used sequenced genomes from eight different GBS isolates to examine this possibility. Researchers compared the genomic sequence data from all these isolates to determine if there were any **conserved genes**—genes that were present and have not changed significantly over time in each isolate—that appeared to be good candidates for a vaccine. Although researchers were unable to identify a single gene that may be a good candidate, they were able to find four genes that were present in the majority of isolates. Based on this information, they predicted that, when combined, they would be present in 87 percent of clinical strains. The researchers also tested the genes in mouse models of disease in order to see if vaccines made from these proteins were effective. Indeed, they found nearly universal protection against all GBS strains that were subsequently used to infect these vaccinated mice.

PILI

It was recently discovered that GBS possess a surface structure called **pili**: stringlike projections made of proteins that extend from the cell surface. Though these haven't been extensively studied in GBS yet, in other bacteria, these pili are used for attachment to host cells and for transfer of DNA between bacteria. Their potential use as a vaccine candidate is discussed in the box below.

BACTERIAL PILI

Pili (singular form is pilus) are bacterial organelles—thin tubes of protein that function in attachment and bacterial "sex" (exchange of genetic material) as well as immune evasion. Traditionally, studies of pili have been carried out in Gram-negative bacteria, such as *Escherichia coli* and *Neisseria* species; very little was known about pili in Gram-positive bacteria. A few recent high-profile papers have changed that.

In July 2005 a group of Italian researchers analyzed two genomes of GBS to identify surface proteins that might be vaccine candidates. Three of the proteins they identified were found to be pilus-like structures extending from the bacterial surface. This was the first-ever description of pili in these bacteria, and it provided a new target for investigation of virulence factors and vaccine candidates, as immunization with these proteins protected mice against a lethal dose of the bacteria.

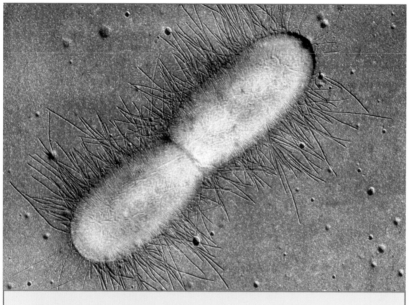

Figure 7.1 An example of pili seen in an *E. coli* bacterium. (CNRI/Photo Researchers, Inc.)

OTHER OPTIONS: PASSIVE IMMUNIZATION

Providing vaccines to very young infants is often a health concern. Because of their immature immune systems, infants don't always respond as well to vaccination as older children do. Vaccines, however, may protect the infant without even being given directly. Some scientists believe that immunizing pregnant women against GBS would also protect the fetus by means of **passive immunization**. That is, the antibodies produced by the mother would circulate in her bloodstream and be passed along to the fetus. It has been estimated that up to 95 percent of GBS infections could be prevented by maternal immunization early in the third trimester of pregnancy. A late-term vaccination, however, would not benefit premature infants—a group that is at high risk for invasive GBS disease. Vaccinating pregnant women is also a difficult proposal. The vaccine must be safe for both the woman and the fetus, and it can be difficult to secure approval for the kinds of tests needed to develop this vaccine. An alternative approach would be to vaccinate adolescents. Using this approach, women would have immunity to GBS before becoming pregnant. Data would first need to be collected to determine how long protective immunity would last, to ensure that immunity would not fade before pregnancy actually took place. Perhaps a booster shot could be provided before beginning a family.

Glossary

aminoglycoside—A class of antibiotics

amnion—The innermost fetal membrane that surrounds the fetus and contains the amniotic fluid

amniotic fluid—A liquid that surrounds and protects the fetus inside the amniotic sac within the uterus

antibiotic—A substance that inhibits or destroys bacteria

antibiotic resistance—A bacterium's ability to avoid being killed by an antibiotic

antibodies—Proteins of the immune system that recognize foreign substances

antigen—A substance that stimulates an immune response

antioxidant—A chemical that prevents the oxidation of other chemicals; found to be protective against a number of cancers in humans

antisera (singular form is *antiserum*)—Blood sera that contains antibodies

asymptomatic—Not showing any overt symptoms or manifestations of disease

bacteremia—The presence of bacteria in the blood

bacteriophage—A virus that infects bacteria

beta-hemolytic—Capable of destroying red blood cells, which causes a clear zone to show up on a blood agar plate

bias—Any deviation of results from the truth, due to poor study design or purposeful misleading

biofilm—A layer of microbes that grows on a surface

blood agar plate—A semisolid, gelatin-like media containing 5 percent sheep blood and a gelatin-like substance used to grow a variety of bacteria

C5a peptidase—A protein produced by group A and B streptococci that cuts the host immune molecule C5

capsule—A sticky outer coating produced by many species of bacteria, including group B streptococci

carbohydrate—A compound, such as a sugar or starch, consisting of carbon, hydrogen, and oxygen

carotenoid—One of a number of yellow-orange pigments

carriage—The presence of a species in the host, irrespective of disease status

case—Someone who is affected by a disease or condition

case-control study—A study that compares those affected by a disease or condition (cases) with those who are not (controls) in order to determine differences in the two populations that may lead to the development of disease

cellulitis—An acute inflammation of the subcutaneous tissues and occasionally muscle, due to an infection

cesarean section—A surgical procedure in which a baby is delivered through an incision in the abdomen rather than through the birth canal

cholera toxin B—A protein that may be linked to carbohydrate antigens in order to make them more antigenic in a vaccine preparation

chorioamniotic space—The area between the two membranes that enclose the fetus—the chorion and the amnion

chorion—An outer membrane surrounding the amnion

cirrhosis—Hardening of the liver

clone—An exact copy

coccus—A type of spherical bacteria

cohort—A group with a common characteristic, studied over time as part of a scientific investigation

coliform—A group of gram-negative bacteria commonly carried in the gut, including *Escherichia coli*

colonize—To establish a presence and replicate in a host

commensal—Living within another organism, but not causing any harm or damage

conserved genes—Genes that have not changed significantly over time

controls—Those who are unaffected by the outcome of interest (for example, the development of a particular disease)

cytokines—Proteins produced by the immune system that act as intracellular mediators

dessication—Drying out

diabetes mellitus—A metabolic disorder that causes a lack of insulin in the body

disease—Sickness or disorder

DNA (deoxyribonucleic acid)—The genetic code of life, made up of individual bases called nucleotides

Glossary

early-onset—Referring to disease caused by *Streptococcus agalactiae* that appears in the first 10 days of life

endocarditis—Inflammation of the lining of the heart and its valves

epidemiologists—Scientists who study the development of disease

epidemiology—The study of the prevalence and spread of disease

flora—The microorganisms that live in the body

genome—The entire DNA sequence of an organism

Gram-negative—A bacterial classification based on the cell wall and membrane structure. Gram-negative bacteria do not retain a dye used for typing, and therefore appear pink after staining.

Gram-positive—A bacterial classification based on the cell wall and membrane structure. Gram-positive bacteria retain a dye used for typing, and therefore appear purple after staining. *Streptococcus agalactiae* is a Gram-positive bacterium.

horizontal gene transfer—The transfer of a gene from one bacterium to another

housekeeping genes—Genes that play a role in critical cellular functions, such as metabolism and DNA repair

hypotension—Low blood pressure

immunocompromised—Having an impaired or weakened immune system

immunogenic—Capable of stimulating the immune system

immunoglobulin—See ANTIBODIES

incidence—The number of new cases of a disease in a given time period

infection—The presence of toxic organisms within the body

intranasally—Through the nose

intrapartum—During the act of labor or delivery

in utero—Before birth, or within the uterus

isolate—A clone that has been recovered from a colonized individual

late-onset—Referring to disease caused by *Streptococcus agalactiae* that occurs in infants between 11 days and three months of age

lateral gene transfer—See HORIZONTAL GENE TRANSFER

lethargic—Tired

lysins—Proteins that break apart cells

lysis—The act of breaking apart a cell

mastitis—Infection of the mammary glands

meningitis—Inflammation of the meninges—the membranes surrounding the brain and spinal cord

mortality rate—The number of people who die of a disease

multi-locus sequence typing (MLST)—A bacterial typing scheme in which housekeeping genes are sequenced and compared to determine relatedness between strains of bacteria

mutations—Inheritable changes in the DNA sequence that can be beneficial, detrimental, or neutral

necrotizing enterocolitis—A severe infection of the gastrointestinal tract that may result in damage to the intestine

necrotizing fasciitis—Also known as flesh-eating disease, it is a severe bacterial infection of the deep skin tissue that is progressive and spreads rapidly

neonate—A newborn infant

neutrophils—Cells of the immune system that engulf and "eat" invading pathogens

nosocomial transmission—The spread of infectious agents within a hospital setting

nucleotides—The building blocks of DNA

otitis media—Inflammation of the inner ear

pan-genome—The complete genetic content of an entire species

passive immunization—Immunity achieved through the transfer of antibodies from an immune individual to a susceptible one—for example, from mother to child during breast-feeding

pathogen—An infectious agent that causes disease symptoms

pathogenesis—The origin of a disease

peptidoglycan—A polymer composed of proteins and polysaccharides that makes up bacterial cell walls

perinatal—Occurring in, concerned with, or being in the period around the time of birth

Glossary

pharyngitis—Inflammation of the throat

phenotype—The physical appearance of an organism

phylogeny—The evolutionary history and relatedness of bacterial species

pili (singular form is *pilus*)—Hair-like structures on the surface of a bacterial cell

pneumonia—A disease of the lungs caused chiefly by infection that is characterized especially by inflammation and is accompanied by fever, chills, cough, and difficulty breathing

polysaccharide—A complex sugar

prophylaxis—A protective or preventive treatment

prospective—Going forward in time

puerperal sepsis—Bacterial infection of the blood following childbirth

pulsed-field gel electrophoresis (PFGE)—A method of typing bacterial strains by cutting their DNA and examining the pattern it produces

quorum sensing—Communication among bacteria through the use of signaling molecules

restriction enzyme—An enzyme used to cut DNA into smaller fragments

retrospective—Looking backward in time

risk factors—Elements that make the development of a particular disease more likely

sepsis—A systemic inflammatory response syndrome induced by a documented infection

septicemia—Invasion of the bloodstream by microorganisms

serotypes—Groups of related microorganisms distinguished by a common set of antigens

shock—Failure to maintain adequate blood volume and flow to organs

side effects—Secondary and usually adverse effects of a treatment

sterile—Free of life

streptococcal toxic shock-like syndrome (STSS)—A condition characterized by the sudden onset of fever, low blood pressure, vomiting, diarrhea, shock, and sometimes a rash

subclinical—See Asymptomatic

subcutaneous—Beneath the skin

surveillance—Close and continuous observation or testing

symptoms—Manifestations of disease

toxin—A substance that is poisonous to the human body

toxoid—A weakened bacterial toxin sometimes used in vaccines

variables—Factors that may change in a study or experiment

vertical transmission—Spread from the mother to the child, generally via the birth canal

virulence factors—Elements or characteristics that allow an organism to cause disease

virulence genes—Genes that help make a bacterium cause disease

zoonotic disease—Disease that is transmitted between animal species

Bibliography

Adderson, E.E., et al. "Subtractive Hybridization Identifies a Novel Predicted Protein Mediating Epithelial Cell Invasion by Virulent Serotype III Group B *Streptococcus agalactiae.*" *Infection and Immunity* 71 (2003): 6857–6863.

Agouridakis, P., et al. " 'Honeymoon' Meningitis." *Emerging Medicine Journal* 22 (2005): 803–804.

Amaya, R.A., et al. "Healthy Elderly People Lack Neutrophil-mediated Functional Activity to Type V Group B Streptococcus." *Journal of the American Geriatric Society* 52 (2004): 46–50.

Anthony, B.F., and K.M. Okada. "The Emergence of Group B Streptococci in Infections of the Newborn Infant." *Streptococci and Streptococcal Diseases*, eds. L.W. Wannamaker and J.M. Matsen. New York: Academic Press, 1972.

Baker, C.J., F.F. Barrett, R.C. Gordon, and M.D. Yow. "Suppurative Meningitis Due to Streptococci of Lancefield Group B: A Study of 33 Infants." *The Journal of Pediatrics* 82 (1973): 724–729.

Baker, C.J., and W.E. Edwards. "Group B Streptococcal Infections." *Infectious Diseases of the Fetus and Newborn Infant*, 4th ed., eds. J.S. Remington and J.O. Klein. (Philadelphia: Saunders, 1995): 980–1054.

Barton, L.L., R.D. Feigin, and R. Lins. "Group B Beta Hemolytic Streptococcal Meningitis in Infants." *The Journal of Pediatrics* 82 (1973): 719–723.

Bisharat, N., et al. "Hyperinvasive Neonatal Group B Streptococcus Has Arisen From a Bovine Ancestor." *Journal of Clinical Microbiology* 42 (2004): 2126–2127.

Blancas, D., et al. "Group B Streptococcal Disease in Nonpregnant Adults: Incidence, Clinical Characteristics, and Outcome." *European Journal of Clinical Microbiology and Infectious Disease.* 23 (2004): 168–173.

Bliss, S.J., et al. "Group B Streptococcus Colonization in Male and Nonpregnant Female University Students: A Cross-sectional Prevalence Study." *Clinical Infectious Diseases* 34 (2002): 184–190.

Bohnsack, J.F., et al. "Phylogenetic Classification of Serotype III Group B Streptococci on the Basis of *hylB* Gene Analysis and DNA Sequences Specific to Restriction Digest Pattern Type III-3." *The Journal of Infectious Diseases* 183 (2001): 1694–1697.

Bohnsack, J.F., et al. "Serotype III *Streptococcus agalactiae* From Bovine Milk and Human Neonatal Infections." *Emerging Infectious Diseases* 10 (2004): 1412–1419.

Chen, K.T., et al. "No Increase in Rates of Early-onset Neonatal Sepsis by Antibiotic-resistant Group B Streptococcus in the Era of Intrapartum Antibiotic Prophylaxis." *American Journal of Obstetrics and Gynecology* 192 (2005): 1167–1171.

Cheng, Q., et al. "Removal of Group B Streptococci Colonizing the Vagina and Oropharynx of Mice With a Bacteriophage Lytic Enzyme." *Antimicrobial Agents and Chemotherapy* 49 (2005): 111–117.

Dermer, P., et al. "A History of Neonatal Group B Streptococcus with Its Related Morbidity and Mortality Rates in the United States." *Journal of Pediatric Nursing* 19 (2004): 357–363.

DiPersio, L.P., and J.R. DiPersio. "High Rates of Erythromycin and Clindamycin Resistance Among OBGYN Isolates of Group B Streptococcus." *Diagnostic Microbiology and Infectious Disease* 54 (2006): 79–82.

Edwards et al. "Group B Streptococcal Colonization and Serotype-specific Immunity in Healthy Elderly Persons." *Clinical Infectious Diseases* 40 (2005): 352–327.

Eickhoff, T.C. "Group B Streptococci in Human Infection." *Streptococci and Streptococcal Diseases*, ed. L.W. Wannamaker and J.M. Matsen. New York: Academic Press, 1972.

Eickhoff, T.C., J.O. Klein, A.D. Daly, et al. "Neonatal Sepsis and Other Infections Due to Group B Beta-hemolytic Streptococci." *New England Journal of Medicine* 271 (1964): 1221.

Ekelund, K., et al. "Emergence of Invasive Serotype VIII Group B Streptococcal Infections in Denmark." *Journal of Clinical Microbiology* 41 (2003): 4442–4444.

Elliott, J.A., et al. "Sudden Increase in Isolation of Group B Streptococci, Serotype V, Is Not Due to Emergence of a New Pulsed-field Gel Electrophoresis Type." *Journal of Clinical Microbiology* 36 (1998): 2115–2116.

Facklam, R. "What Happened to the Streptococci: Overview of Taxonomic and Nomenclature Changes." *Clinical Microbiology Reviews* 15 (2002): 613–630.

Feldman, R.G. "Toward a Universal Multistrain Bacterial Vaccine." *Nature Biotechnology* 23 (2005): 1087–1088.

Fortin, M., and R. Higgins. "Mixed Infection Associated with a Group B Streptococcus in a Dog." *Canadian Veterinary Journal* 42 (2001): 730.

Franciosi, R.A., et al. "Group B Streptococcal Neonatal and Infant Infections." *The Journal of Pediatrics* 82 (1973): 707–718.

Franciosi, R.A., et al. "Group B Streptococcal Neonatal and Infant Infections." *The Journal of Pediatrics* 135 (1973): 392–397.

Fry, R.M. "Fatal Infections by Haemolytic Streptococcus Group B." *The Lancet* 1 (1938): 199–201.

Gardman, M.A., et al. "Group B Streptococcal Necrotizing Fasciitis and Streptococcal Toxic Shock-like Syndrome in Adults." *Archives of Internal Medicine* 158 (1998): 1704–1708.

Glasgow, T.S., et al. "Association of Intrapartum Antibiotic Exposure and Late-onset Serious Bacterial Infections in Infants." *Pediatrics* 116 (2005): 696–702.

Guihot, A., et al. "Group B Streptococcal Meningitis in a Patient with Horizontal Transmission: Beware of Toothbrushing on Sunday Mornings." *Journal of Infection* 50 (2005): 240–241.

Gutekunst, H., et al. "Analysis of RogB-controlled Virulence Mechanisms and Gene Expression in *Streptococcus agalactiae*." *Infection and Immunity* 71 (2003): 5056–5064.

Hare, R., and L. Colebrook. "The Biochemical Reactions of Hemolytic Streptococci from the Vagina of Febrile and Afebrile Parturient Women." *Journal of Pathology and Bacteriology* 39 (1934): 429-442.

Hetzel, U., et al. "Septicaemia in Emerald Monitors (*Varanus prasinus* Schlegel 1839) Caused by *Streptococcus agalactiae* Acquired from Mice." *Veterinary Microbiology* 95 (2003): 283–293.

Hickman, M.E., et al. "Changing Epidemiology of Group B Streptococcal Colonization." *Pediatrics* 104 (1999): 203–209.

Hoffman, D.J., and M.C. Harris. "Diagnosis of Neonatal Sepsis." *Intensive Care of the Fetus and Newborn*, ed. A.R. Spritzer. (Mosby, Minneapolis: 1996): 940–950.

Hood, M., A. Janney, and G. Dameron. "Beta Hemolytic Streptococcus Group B Associated with Problems of the Perinatal Period." *American Journal of Obstetrics and Gynecology* 82 (1961): 809–818.

Jiang, S-M., et al. "Regulation of Virulence by a Two-component System in Group B Streptococcus." *Journal of Bacteriology* 187 (2005): 1105–1113.

Karin, Brigtsen A., et al. "Induction of Cross-reactive Antibodies by Immunization of Healthy Adults with Types Ia and Ib Group B

Streptococcal Polysaccharide-tetanus Toxoid Conjugate Vaccines." *The Journal of Infectious Diseases* 185 (2002): 1277–84.

Keet, D.F., et al. "Ulcerative Pododermatitis in Free-ranging African Elephant (*Loxodonta africana*) in the Kruger National Park." *The Onderstepoort Journal of Veterinary Research* 64 (1997): 25–32.

Kenyon, S.L., et al. "Broad-spectrum Antibiotics for Preterm, Prelabour Rupture of Fetal Membranes: The ORACLE I Randomized Trial." *Lancet* 357 (2001): 979–988.

Kenyon, S.L., et al. "Broad-spectrum Antibiotics for Spontaneous Preterm Labor: The ORACLE II Randomized Trial." *Lancet* 357 (2001): 989–994.

Kornblatt, A.N., et al. "Canine Neonatal Deaths Associated with Group B Streptococcal Septicemia." *Journal of the American Veterinary Medical Association* 183 (1983): 700–701.

Lämmler, C., et al. "Properties of Serological Group B Streptococci of Dog, Cat, and Monkey Origin." *Journal of Veterinary Medicine, Series B* 45 (1998): 561–566.

Lamy, M.C., et al. "CovS/CovR of Group B Streptococcus: A Two-component Global Regulatory System Involved in Virulence." *Molecular Microbiology* 54 (2004): 1250–1268.

Lancefield, R.C. "A Serological Differentiation of Human and Other Groups of Hemolytic Streptococci." *The Journal of Experimental Medicine* 57 (1933): 571–595.

———. "A Serological Differentiation of Specific Types of Bovine Hemolytic Streptococci (Group B)." *The Journal of Experimental Medicine* 59 (1934): 441–448.

Larsson, C., et al. "Intranasal Immunization of Mice with Group B Streptococcal Protein Rib and Cholera Toxin B Subunit Confers Protection Against Lethal Infection." *Infection and Immunity* 72 (2004): 1184–1187.

Lauer, P., et al. "Genome Analysis Reveals Pili in Group B *Streptococcus*." *Science* 309 (2005): 105.

Lee, N.Y., et al. "Group B Streptococcal Soft Tissue Infections in Non-pregnant Adults." *Clinical Microbiology and Infection* 11 (2005): 577–579.

Lindahl, G., et al. "Surface Proteins of *Streptococcus agalactiae* and Related Proteins in Other Bacterial Pathogens." *Clinical Microbiology Reviews* 18 (2005): 102–107.

Bibliography

Liu, G.Y., et al. "Extracellular Virulence Factors of Group B Streptococci." *Frontiers in Bioscience* 9 (2004): 1794–1802.

Liu, G.Y., et al. "Sword and Shield: Linked Group B Streptococcal ß-hemolysin/cytolysin and Carotenoid Pigment Function to Subvert Host Phagocyte Defense." *Proceedings of the National Academy of Sciences* 101 (2004): 14491–14496.

Malone, D., et al. "Identification of a Universal Group B *Streptococcus* Vaccine by Multiple Genome Screen." *Science* 309 (2005): 148–150.

Manning, S.D., et al. "Correlates of Antibiotic-resistant Group B Streptococcus Isolated from Pregnant Women." *Journal of the American College of Obstetricians and Gynecologists* 101 (2003): 74–79.

Manning, S.D., et al. "Determinants of Co-colonization with Group B Streptococcus Among Heterosexual College Couples." *Epidemiology* 13 (2002): 533–539.

Manning, S.D., et al. "Frequency of Antibiotic Resistance Among Group B Streptococcus Isolated from Healthy College Students." *Clinical Infectious Diseases* 33 (2001): 137–139.

Manning, S.D., et al. "Prevalence of Group B Streptococcus Colonization and Potential for Transmission by Casual Contact in Healthy Young Men and Women." *Clinical Infectious Diseases* 39 (2004): 280–288.

Martin, D., et al. "Protection from Group B Streptococcal Infection in Neonatal Mice by Maternal Immunization With Recombinant Sip Protein." *Infection and Immunity* 70 (2002): 4897–4901.

McCracken, G.H. "Group B Streptococci: The New Challenge in Neonatal Infections." *Journal of Pediatrics* 82 (1973): 703–706.

Messier, M., et al. "*Streptococcus agalactiae* Endocarditis with Embolization in a Dog." *Canadian Veterinary Journal* 36 (1995): 703–704.

Meyn, L.A., et al. "Association of Sexual Activity with Colonization and Vaginal Acquisition of Group B Streptococcus in Nonpregnant Women." *American Journal of Epidemiology* 155 (2002): 949–957.

Mikamo, H., et al. "Adherence to, Invasion by, and Cytokine Production in Response to Serotype VIII Group B Streptococci." *Infection and Immunity* 72 (2004): 4716–4722.

Mora, M., et al. "Group A *Streptococcus* Produce Pilus-like Structures Containing Protective Antigens and Lancefield T Antigens." *Proceedings of the National Academy of Science* 102 (2005): 15641–15646.

Mullaney, D.M. "Group B Streptococcal Infections in Newborns." *Journal of Obstetric, Gynecologic, and Neonatal Nursing* 30 (2001): 649–658.

Musser, J.M., et al. "Identification of a High-virulence Clone of Type III *Streptococcus agalactiae* (Group B Streptococcus) Causing Invasive Neonatal Disease." *Proceedings of the National Academy of Sciences USA* 86 (1989): 4731–4735.

Norcard, M. Mollereau. "Sur une mammite contagieuse des vaches liatieres." (on contagious mastitis of milk cows) *Annals of the Pasteur Institute* 1 (1887): 109.

Olson, M.E., et al. "Biofilm Bacteria: Formation and Comparative Susceptibility to Antibiotics." *The Canadian Journal of Veterinary Medicine* 66 (2002): 86–92.

Palacios, G.C., et al. "Identification of the High-virulence Clone of Group B Streptococci in Mexican Isolates by Growth Characteristics at 40 Degrees C." *Current Microbiology* 38 (1999): 126–131.

Palazzi, D.L., et al. "Use of Type V Group B Streptococcal Conjugate Vaccine in Adults 65–85 Years Old." *Journal of Infectious Disease* 190 (2004): 558–564.

Paoletti, L.J., et al. "A Serotype VIII Strain Among Colonizing Group B Streptococcal Isolates in Boston, Massachusetts." *Journal of Clinical Microbiology* 37 (1999): 3759–3760.

Pasnik, D.J., et al. "Antigenicity of *Streptococcus agalactiae* Extracellular Products and Vaccine Efficacy." *Journal of Fish Diseases* 28 (2005): 205–212.

Pearlman, M.D., et al. "Frequent Resistance of Clinical Group B Streptococcal Isolates to Clindamycin and Erythromycin." *Obstetrics and Gynecology* 92 (1998): 258–261.

Pritzlaff, C.A., et al. "Genetic Basis for the ß-haemolytic/cytolytic Activity of Group B Streptococcus." *Molecular Microbiology* 39 (2001): 236–247.

Reich, H.L., et al. "Group B Streptococcal Toxic Shock-like Syndrome." *Archives of Dermatology* 140 (2004): 163–166.

Rench, M.A., and C.J. Baker. "Neonatal Sepsis Caused by a New Group B Streptococcal Serotype." *Journal of Pediatrics* 122 (1993): 638–640.

Rouse, D.J., et al. "Antibiotic Susceptibility Profile of Group B Streptococcus Acquired Vertically." *Obstetrics and Gynecology* 92 (1998): 931–934.

Sater, K.J. "Treatment of Sepsis in the Neonate." *Journal of Intravenous Nursing* 21 (1998): 275–281.

Schoening, T.E., et al. "Prevalence of Erythromycin and Clindamycin Resistance Among *Streptococcus agalactiae* Isolates in Germany." *Clinical Microbiology and Infection* 11 (2005): 577–596.

Schrag, S.J., et al. "Group B Streptococcal Disease in the Era of Intrapartum Antibiotic Prophylaxis." *New England Journal of Medicine* 342 (2000): 15–20.

Schuchat, A. "Epidemiology of Group B Streptococcal Disease in the United States: Shifting Paradigms." *Clinical Microbiology Reviews* 11 (1998): 497–513.

Shen, X., et al. "Preparation and Preclinical Evaluation of Experimental Group B Streptococcus Type III Polysaccharide-cholera Toxin B Subunit Conjugate Vaccine for Intranasal Immunization." *Vaccine* 19 (2001): 850–861.

Takahashi, et al. "Identification of a Highly Encapsulated, Genetically Related Group of Invasive Type III Group B Streptococci." *Journal of Infectious Diseases* 177 (1998): 1116–1119.

Tettelin, H., et al. "Genome Analysis of Multiple Pathogenic Isolates of *Streptococcus agalactiae*: Implications for the Microbial 'Pan-genome.' " *Proceedings of the National Academy of Science* 102 (2005): 13950–13955.

Wong, C.H., et al. "Group B Streptococcus Necrotizing Fasciitis: An Emerging Disease?" *European Journal of Clinical Infectious Disease* 23 (2004): 573–575.

Yildirim, A.O., et al. "Identification and Characterization of *Streptococcus agalactiae* Isolated from Horses." *Veterinary Microbiology* 85 (2002): 31–35.

Yildirim, A.O., et al. "Pheno- and Genotypic Properties of Streptococci of Serological Group B of Canine and Feline Origin." *FEMS Microbiology Letters* 212 (2002): 187–192.

Younan, M., et al. "Application of the California Mastitis Test in Intramammary *Streptococcus agalactiae* and *Staphylococcus aureus* Infections of Camels (*Camelus dromedaries*) in Kenya." *Preventative Veterinary Medicine* 51 (2001): 307–316.

Zangwill, K.M., et al. "Group B Streptococcal Disease in the United States, 1990: Report from a Multistate Active Surveillance System." *Morbidity and Mortality Weekly Reports CDC Surveillance Summary* 41 (1992): 25–32.

Web Sites

Aetiology
http://scienceblogs.com/aetiology
Discussion of infectious disease epidemiology, including *Streptococcus agalactiae.*

Centers for Disease Control and Prevention (CDC)
http://www.cdc.gov

Emerging Infectious Diseases Journal Homepage
http://www.cdc.gov/ncidod/EID/index.htm

Group B Strep Disease
http://www.cdc.gov/groupbstrep/

Group B Streptococcal Disease (GBS)
http://www.cdc.gov/ncidod/dbmd/diseaseinfo/groupbstrep_g.htm

Group B Streptococcus
http://www.astdhpphe.org/infect/strepb.html

Streptococcus Group B Infections
http://www.emedicine.com/MED/topic2185.htm

Index

Index

About the Author

Tara C. Smith, Ph.D., obtained her B.S. in biology from Yale University, where she carried out research on the molecular epidemiology of *Streptococcus pyogenes*. In 2002 she earned her Ph.D. at the Medical University of Ohio in Toledo, studying microbial pathogenesis and virulence factor regulation in *Streptococcus pyogenes* (group A streptococcus). She completed post-doctoral training in molecular epidemiology of *Streptococcus agalactiae* (group B streptococcus) at the University of Michigan. Dr. Smith is currently an assistant professor at the University of Iowa. Her current research centers on investigation of hypervariable proteins in *S. agalactiae*. Other current projects involve studying the epidemiology and molecular biology of *E. coli*, *Streptococcus suis*, and influenza. Additional interests include microbial ecology, emerging diseases, zoonoses, and infectious causes of chronic disease. Dr. Smith is also the mother of two children and lives near Iowa City, Iowa.

About the Editor

The late I. Edward Alcamo was a Distinguished Teaching Professor of Microbiology at the State University of New York at Farmingdale. Alcamo studied biology at Iona College in New York and earned his M.S. and Ph.D. degrees in microbiology at St. John's University, also in New York. He had taught at Farmingdale for more than 30 years. In 2000, Alcamo won the Carski Award for Distinguished Teaching in Microbiology, the highest honor for microbiology teachers in the United States. He was a member of the American Society for Microbiology, the National Association of Biology teachers, and the American Medical Writers Association. Alcamo authored numerous books on the subjects of microbiology, AIDS, and DNA technology as well as the award-winning textbook *Fundamentals of Microbiology*, now in its sixth edition.